FOR KING AND EMPIRE

THE CANADIANS AT

PASSCHENDAELE,

October to November 1917

A Social History and Battlefield Tour

by N. M. Christie

edited by S. Hickman

© NORM CHRISTIE

For King and Empire
Volume: IV
The Canadians at Passchendaele
October to November 1917

ISBN 0-9699039-7-9

Copyright 1996
1. Military   2. First World War   3. Canada

Published by: Bunker to Bunker Books
                     34 Blue Spruce Cres.
                     Winnipeg, MB. R2M 4C2

Distributed by: C.E.F. Books   Bunker to Bunker Books
                     P.O. Box 29123   34 Blue Spruce Cres.
                     3500 Fallowfield Rd.   Winnipeg,
                     Nepean,   MB, R2M 4C2
                     ON K2J 4A9

Other Books in the Series

Volume I: The Canadians at Ypres, 22nd–26th April 1915

Volume II: The Canadians on the Somme, September–November 1916

Volume III: The Canadians at Vimy, April 1917

Volume V: The Canadians at Arras and the Drocourt-Queant Line,
                 August–September 1918

Volume VI: The Canadians at the Canal-du-Nord and Cambrai,
                 September–October 1918

Volume VII: The Canadians at Amiens, August 1918

Front cover picture: Photo by Susan Hickman

Back cover picture: Talbot Mercer Papineau, MC, April 1916 (PAC C013222)

Printed in Canada

This book is dedicated to my father

Norman Radcliffe Christie

Warrant Officer (Pilot) Royal Canadian Air Force

United Kingdom 1944

India and Burma 1945 (215 (RAF) and 117 (RAF) Squadrons)

YOUR KING AND COUNTRY NEED *THEM*

IF YOU KNOW OF ANY MEN WHO OUGHT TO ENLIST WON'T YOU USE YOUR INFLUENCE TO HAVE THEM ENLIST AT ONCE?

PLEASE RE-ENCLOSE THIS WHEN WRITING TO ONE OF YOUR ENGLISH-SPEAKING CORRESPONDENTS IN THE PROVINCE OF QUEBEC OR EASTERN ONTARIO.

PLEASE SEE OTHER SIDE

CITIZENS'
RECRUITING ASSOCIATION
McGill Building, Montreal

TABLE OF CONTENTS

Introduction 1

Getting There 3

What to Bring 4

About Ypres (Ieper) 5

Components of the Canadian Expeditionary Force 10

The Battlefield - Defences and Conditions 13

The Battle of Passchendaele: Historical Overview 15

Tour Itinerary 27

The Tour 28

Cemeteries and Memorials 53

The Body Snatchers 66

Canadian Indians 70

Is It Nothing 74

Further Reference 80

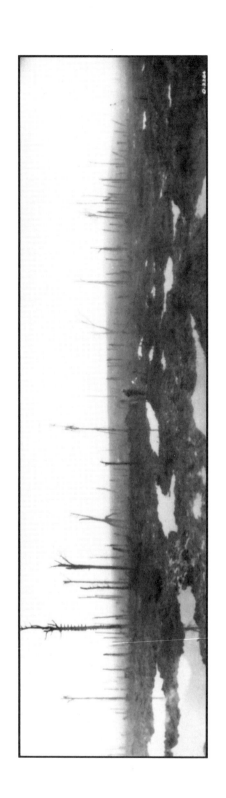

The desolation of the Passchendaele battlefield

INTRODUCTION
THE BATTLE OF PASSCHENDAELE 1917
(Third Battle of Ypres)

Passchendaele represents the horror and the futility that was the Great War. A repulsive battle where wounded soldiers drowned in the mud, where artillery sank and where men attacked in unfathomable conditions for reasons we find hard to grasp, Passchendaele was hell on earth.

The Canadians entered the battle in October 1917, almost three months after the first attacks of July 31, 1917. The British and Australians had paid with more than 250,000 casualties for an advance of only 5,500 metres.

The few Canadian veterans who remained after the fighting in the Ypres Salient in 1915 and 1916 did not recognize the place. Ypres itself had been obliterated by the continuous bombardment and the flat farmland had become a morass of mud, shell holes and corpses. The pervading smell of the dead is a memory of most Great War veterans who served there. Greenery was absent and only splinters remained where forests had once stood. Ypres was utter desolation.

When the Canadians arrived to take their turn in the meat grinder, the objective to secure the heights surrounding Ypres and break through to the channel ports had been abandoned. The campaign had turned into a hideous battle of attrition, with the Germans, as always, holding the best positions.

Most of the Canadians who fought there in 1915 and 1916 were wounded or now lay in graves on the Somme or at Vimy. These new Canadians of 1917 were 'Byng's Boys,' the Canadians of Vimy, the most successful Corps in the British army. Experienced, organized and proud, they had worked hard to achieve their reputation as storm troops. They had succeeded at Vimy, Arleux, Fresnoy and Hill 70, all great victories in 1917. Now, in October, they faced a formidable challenge.

Fighting on into November, achieving a victory few thought possible, the Canadian Corps would capture and hold the heights of Passchendaele Ridge, an advance of a little more than 2,000 metres.

It would take the Corps' full resources of 100,000 men three weeks to capture it. Five thousand would die.

In the German commander's own words, they "charged like a wild bull against the iron wall which kept him from our submarine bases."

Today we know little of Passchendaele. Most of the ferocious memories of that battle have been buried with the veterans who fought there. For us who remain, it is part of our heritage, the work of generations gone before, men who fought with tenacity and courage to bring pride to Canada today.

The objective of this volume, and the other volumes in this series, is to bring to Canadians an understanding of the achievements of our grandfathers and to know, with pride, what they accomplished.

The quotation which best tells of Passchendaele was made by Major Talbot Papineau MC of the Princess Patricia's Canadian Light Infantry to a fellow officer before the attack of October 30, 1917. "You know Hughie. This is suicide." Papineau was killed instantly a few minutes later.

Remember when you tour this battlefield and observe the small area over which the battle took place, that for this ground, 11,000 Canadians were wounded and 5,000 died.

GETTING THERE

Ypres or Ieper (as it is now called) is located in western Belgium, 20 kilometres north of the Belgian/French border. It is easily accessible from Paris (300 kilometres north) and Brussels (100 kilometres). From London, it is a two-hour drive to Dover, a 75-minute ferry ride to Calais, and a 45-minute drive from Calais. The opening of the Channel Tunnel has made a direct rail link from London to Lille, France, which is close to the Belgian border. Check with the Tourist Board for details. Rental cars are available in any of the above-mentioned cities and tourist offices can supply routes and details of hotels.

In Belgium, the main language is Flemish, an accented version of Dutch. About a third of Belgians speak French, which was the country's official language for centuries. However, as Flanders became richer and more industrialized and Flemish nationalism acquired more political clout, the Dutch language was accorded more and more official respect. In 1962, Brussels was made officially bilingual as a concession to the northerners. Belgians in general today speak several languages and English is widely understood.

There are approximately 24 Belgian francs (1996) to one Canadian dollar. In Ypres, French francs are also accepted in most stores and restaurants. Credit cards, such as VISA, Access or MasterCard are accepted, but please check with the hotel where you are staying. Always visit the Tourism Office to obtain information on accommodation or events of interest.

The following tour is based on staying in Ypres and departing from the Grote Markt or town square. However, if the Ypres battlefield tour is part of a larger itinerary, I recommend Arras, France, as another good base of operation. Although English is generally spoken in the main hotels of Arras, otherwise very little English is spoken. Brush up on your French before going.

In France, stores close between noon and 2:00 p.m. always. Be sure to obtain film and other necessities before closing! Stopping for a long lunch is a strict and revered tradition in continental Europe.

There are 3.8 French francs (1996) to one Canadian dollar.

Currency and traveler's checks can be exchanged at any bank.

WHAT TO BRING

Weather is very changeable in this part of Europe. Days can start sunny and change quickly to rain, hail or even a sprinkling of snow. Above all, be prepared for wet weather. For example, the average temperature in Belgium in July varies from 12 to 24ºC. Other than the obvious passport, traveler's checks and appropriate clothing, bring the following to ensure a successful trip:

- a bottle opener and cork screw

- binoculars

- a camera (with 100 and 200 ASA film)

- a compass

- rubber boots

- National Geographic Institute maps 1:25,000, numbers 28/1-2, 28/3-4 and 28/5-6 (these can be obtained at the Tourist Office in Ypres)

- Michelin map No. 51 (preferably the Commonwealth War Graves Commission overprint, showing all the cemeteries)

- reference books (do your research before departure)

ABOUT YPRES

Ypres (Ieper, Ypern) lies in the quiet, picturesque poppy fields of Flanders in western Belgium. Surrounded by hills, lakes and hop fields, this now-modern town has been one of Europe's strategic battlegrounds for centuries. Throughout its 1000-year history, Ypres has always been a tempting prize and military strong point for its neighbors.

In the Middle Ages, the town was one of Belgium's jewels, the strength and wealth of Flanders. A centre of culture and commerce and a flourishing textile trade, Ypres was at its peak in the 13th century with a population of 40,000 with another 150,000 in the surrounding region.

It was at this time construction of the town's most famous building, the great Lakenhalle (Cloth Hall), a monument to Ypres' textile industry, was begun. Taking 100 years to build, this impressive covered market allowed ships to moor alongside to load and discharge cargoes onto a covered quay along the banks of the Yperlee. The Nieuwerck (Town Hall), now a tourist office, was completed some 300 years later. The upper storey, once used for storage, today houses two museums and a concert hall. From its 70-metre belfry, the hours are sounded by a 49-bell carillon.

Ypres' flourishing trade dropped significantly in 1383, when the town was attacked by troops from England and Ghent. Although Ypres resisted the siege, many weavers left, taking the livelihood of the town with them. By the 1500s, the population of the town was 5,000 and its importance had diminished.

Over the last 600 years, Ypres has been attacked by Spaniards, French, Austrians and Dutch. When Ypres became French in 1678, the city's defence works were revamped by renowned French military engineer Marshal Vauban. The six gates were reduced to four. These defences were able to withstand the wars of 1689-1712, but the end of the 18th century witnessed the rebuilding and dismantling of many of the town's defences. In 1815, prior to Waterloo, all exterior works were quickly reconstructed and defended by British troops. After Waterloo, when Belgium united with the Netherlands, Ypres again strongly fortified against any possible French invasion. In the 1830s, when Belgium was granted independence, Ypres

The ruins of the Cathedral and Cloth Hall, Ypres. November 1917

Cloth Hall, Ypres, Market Day 1920

became Belgian and soon afterwards the Belgian government decided Ypres no longer needed to be fortified and levelled all the outer works. Walls and ramparts were removed to make room for railways and old gates demolished to allow wider passage on the roads.

The only gate left, still part of the original French walls, is the Lille Gate or Rijselsepoort at the southern extreme of town.

Where the Menin Gate stands today on the town's eastern flank, in memory of the missing of the First World War, once was graced by the town's most beautiful gate. The Antwerp Gate was refashioned into the Corne d'Anveers by Vauban and named after Napoleon when he visited Ypres in 1804 and an imperial eagle carved into the stonework.

In 1914, Ypres once again lay in the path of warring nations. The German cavalry rode into the town on October 13. The Burgomaster was held to ransom for 75,000 Bfr, but the British Expeditionary Force reached the town the next day and occupied it entirely. The great artillery barrage which began on November 22 damaged ancient buildings and set the Cloth Hall on fire. Civilians suffered considerably and were finally evacuated on May 9, 1915 during the Second Battle of Ypres, when the Cloth Hall, Collegiate Church of St. Martin and other important buildings were destroyed. Although many returned to the ruins of their homes during the comparative quiet of 1916, Ypres was essentially in military hands until the Third Battle of Ypres in 1917. In the spring of 1918, Ypres was nearly lost to the Germans, but the British lines held and the final Allied advance relieved the town, ousting the last German troops September 28.

Belgium was again a trampling ground for occupying German forces in the Second World War. Damage from both wars was so catastrophic that much of the country had to be rebuilt from scratch. Ypres was built from the bottom up after the First World War.

Prominent in Ypres today are its refashioned St. Martin's Cathedral, the towering Cloth Hall and reconstructed 17th-century façades along many streets. The Grote Markt (Great Market) is the town centre and is surrounded by the Courthouse, the old Town Hall, the Kasselrijgebouw (with seven deadly sins carved on its façade) and numerous cafés and restaurants where you can enjoy a beer, a coffee or a good lunch. Market day is Saturday morning.

Prices for food and accommodation in Belgium are generally steep. There are good relais (inns) in the countryside where you can spend the night and have lunch or dinner. Book ahead for a room in a hotel or a relais and make reservations for meals. The tourist office is in the Cloth Hall (tel. 57 200724) and offers comprehensive tourist information in English, as well as guidebooks, maps and leaflets listing hotels and restaurants.

Here is a list of hotels, restaurants, museums and special events to get you started:

Four-star hotels include *Hotel Ariane,* Slachthuisstraat 58 (near Grote Markt), 8900 Ieper, tel. 57 218218; *Hotel Rabbit,* Industrielaan 19, 8900 Ieper, tel. 57 217000; *Regina Hotel,* Grote Markt 45, 8900 Ieper, tel. 57 218888.

Some three-star hotels are *Kasteelhof 't Hooghe,* Meenseweg 481, 8902 Ieper, tel. 57 468787; *Hotel Sultan,* Grote Markt 33, 8900 Ieper, tel. 57 219030.

Some restaurants to consider are *Hostellerie St. Nicolas,* G. de Stuersstraat 6 (near Grote Markt), 8900 Ieper, tel. 57 200622 (some rooms available also); *Gasthof 't Zweerd,* Grote Markt 2, 8900 Ieper, tel. 57 200475 (some rooms); *Restaurant Den Anker,* Grote Markt 30, 8900 Ieper, tel. 57 201272 (restaurant/tea-room); 't Eilandje, Eiland 2, 8900 Ieper, tel. 57 200528 (brasserie/tea-room/restaurant); *'t Hooge,* Meenseweg 467, 8902 Ieper, tel. 57 468446 (this is a café housed in a rebuilt school next to the Hooge Crater Museum); *Restaurant De Palingbeek,* Palingbeekstraat 18, 8902 Ieper, tel. 57 205672; *Restaurant De Steenen Haan,* Komenseweg 21, 8902 Ieper, tel. 57 205486; *De Wijngaard,* Mk. Fochlaan 8, 8900 Ieper, tel. 57 204230 (restaurant/steakhouse); *Zillebekevijver,* Zillebekevijverdreef 2, 8902 Zillebeke, tel. 57 200086 (tavern/tea room).

You might want to check out some of the following museums. Note, most museums are open from 9:30 a.m. to noon and 1:30 to 5:30 p.m. and closed on Mondays, but check with the individual museum:*Educational Museum,* Cloth Hall, Grote Markt, 8900 Ieper, tel. 57 200724, open April 1-October 31; *Remembrance Museum "Ypres Salient '14-'18",* Cloth Hall, Grote Markt, 8900 Ieper, tel. 57 200724, open April 1-November 15; *Museum Merghelynck,* A. Merghelynckstraat 2, 8900 Ieper, tel. 57 203042, open April 1-October 30; *Belle Museum,* Rijselsestraat 38, 8900 Ieper, tel. 57 204831, open April 1-October 30; *Stedelijk (Municipal) Museum,* Ieperleestraat 31, 8900 Ieper, tel. 57 218300, open April 1-October 30; *Hooge Crater 14-18 Museum,* Meenseweg 467, 8902 Zillebeke, tel. 57 468446, open April 1-November 31; *Hill 60-Queen Victoria Rifles Museum,* Zwarteleenstraat 40, 8902 Zillebeke, tel. 57 206276; *Hill 62-Sanctuary Wood Museum,* Canadalaan 26, 8902 Zillebeke, tel. 57 466373.

The principal event of the year in Ypres is Kattenwoensdag or the Cat Festival, which takes place the second Sunday of May. Based on the mediaeval belief that evil spirits adopted the physical form of a cat, cats were widely persecuted and killed. Today, plush toy cats are thrown from the belfry by the festival jester. Until 1817, live cats were thrown.

Every three years, a Parade of Cats honors the animal as portrayed in literature and folklore (next parade 1997). Thousands of costumed revellers take part in the festival.

This guide uses place names of the 1914-18 period. Below is a list of place names as you will see them today (on the left) and as they were known during the war (on the right).

New	Old
Sint-Jan	St. Jean
Ieper	Ypres
Poelkapelle	Poelcapelle
Fortuinhoek	Fortuin
Roeselare	Roulers
Wieltje	Wieltje
Sint-Juliaan	St. Julien
Kerselaar	Keerselaere
Langemark	Langemarck
Pilkem	Pilckem
's-Graventafel	Gravenstafel
Passendale	Passchendaele
Zonnebeke	Zonnebeke
Frezenberg	Frezenberg
Westhoek	Westhoek
Poperinge	Poperinghe

COMPONENTS OF THE CANADIAN EXPEDITIONARY FORCE
PASSCHENDAELE 1917

1ST CANADIAN DIVISION

1ST INFANTRY BRIGADE	2ND INFANTRY BRIGADE	3RD INFANTRY BRIGADE
1ST BATTALION (WESTERN ONTARIO)	5TH BATTALION (SASKATCHEWAN)	13TH BATTALION (BLACK WATCH OF MONTREAL)
2ND BATTALION (EASTERN ONTARIO)	7TH BATTALION (BRITISH COLUMBIA)	14TH BATTALION (ROYAL MONTREAL REGIMENT)
3RD BATTALION (TORONTO REGIMENT)	8TH BATTALION (90TH RIFLES OF WINNIPEG)	15TH BATTALION (48TH HIGHLANDERS OF TORONTO)
4TH BATTALION (CENTRAL ONTARIO)	10TH BATTALION (ALBERTA)	16TH BATTALION (CANADIAN SCOTTISH)

2ND CANADIAN DIVISION

4TH INFANTRY BRIGADE	5TH INFANTRY BRIGADE	6TH INFANTRY BRIGADE
18TH BATTALION (WESTERN ONTARIO)	22ND BATTALION (CANADIEN-FRANÇAIS)	27TH BATTALION (CITY OF WINNIPEG)
19TH BATTALION (CENTRAL ONTARIO)	24TH BATTALION (VICTORIA RIFLES OF MONTREAL)	28TH BATTALION (SASKATCHEWAN)
20TH BATTALION (CENTRAL ONTARIO)	25TH BATTALION (NOVA SCOTIA)	29TH BATTALION (BRITISH COLUMBIA)
21ST BATTALION (EASTERN ONTARIO)	26TH BATTALION (NEW BRUNSWICK)	31ST BATTALION (ALBERTA)

3RD CANADIAN DIVISION

7TH INFANTRY BRIGADE	8TH INFANTRY BRIGADE	9TH INFANTRY BRIGADE
ROYAL CANADIAN REGIMENT (NOVA SCOTIA)	1ST CANADIAN MOUNTED RIFLES (SASKATCHEWAN)	43RD BATTALION (CAMERON HIGHLANDERS OF WINNIPEG)
PRINCESS PATRICIA'S CANADIAN LIGHT INFANTRY (EASTERN ONTARIO)	2ND CANADIAN MOUNTED RIFLES (BRITISH COLUMBIA)	52ND BATTALION (NEW ONTARIO)
42ND BATTALION (BLACK WATCH OF MONTREAL)	4TH CANADIAN MOUNTED RIFLES (CENTRAL ONTARIO)	58TH BATTALION (CENTRAL ONTARIO)
49TH BATTALION (ALBERTA)	5TH CANADIAN MOUNTED RIFLES (QUEBEC)	116TH BATTALION (ONTARIO COUNTY)

4TH CANADIAN DIVISION

10TH INFANTRY BRIGADE	11TH INFANTRY BRIGADE	12TH INFANTRY BRIGADE
44TH BATTALION (MANITOBA)	54TH BATTALION (BRITISH COLUMBIA)	38TH BATTALION (EASTERN ONTARIO)
46TH BATTALION (SASKATCHEWAN)	75TH BATTALION (MISSISSAUGA HORSE)	72ND BATTALION (SEAFORTH HIGHLANDERS OF VANCOUVER)
47TH BATTALION (BRITISH COLUMBIA)	87TH BATTALION (GRENADIER GUARDS OF MONTREAL)	78TH BATTALION (WINNIPEG GRENADIERS)
50TH BATTALION (ALBERTA)	102ND BATTALION (NORTH BRITISH COLUMBIANS)	85TH BATTALION (NOVA SCOTIA HIGHLANDERS)

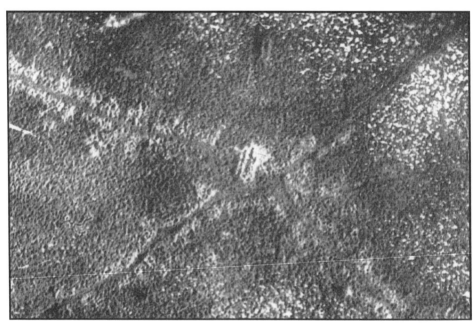

Aerial photographs of Passchendaele village before and after the battle. The church can be distinguished at the road junction.

THE BATTLEFIELD - DEFENCES AND CONDITIONS

THE GERMAN DEFENCES

To understand the conditions and the strategy of this battle, the defences at Ypres must be explained. Because the high water table precluded the use of traditional trenches used on the Somme or at Vimy, the Germans used a complex system of interlocking pill-boxes. This system was best described by S. G. Bennett, historian of the 4th Canadian Mounted Rifles:

"The enemy's line of defence was not a series of uniform trenches to be taken and mopped up. Instead there were isolated trenches and strong-points dotted here and there. The greatest obstacles were the pill-boxes. They were manned by picked resistance-troops who fought with courage and resolution, keeping their rifles and machine-guns in action until bombed or bayoneted. Only by collective bravery and individual acts of gallantry were these obstacles removed. Contrary to popular belief the majority of pill-boxes were not loop-holed fortresses from which the defenders fought. They were square rooms of reinforced-concrete with walls and roof about five feet thick with one door in the rear leading into a fire-trench. Their walls were too thick to allow a field of fire through ports. During a bombardment and when not in action, the garrison gained shelter within, but as soon as an attack was launched, the occupants manned the fire-trench which ran behind and extended on either side of the pill-box. They took the place of deep dug-outs, which were impracticable in such a low-lying country and were good rallying points giving moral support to the defenders.

"They were formidable, but with one weakness, their range of fire was limited, and unless covered by other pill-boxes on the flanks the blind points in the range of fire made it possible for individual attackers to crawl up under cover and bomb the garrison behind. This explains many of the individual acts of heroism in capturing or demolishing a crew defending a pillbox."

THE CONDITIONS

The summer of 1917 in this sodden part of Europe had its typical dose of heavy precipitation. Add to that the destruction of the existing drainage system by prolonged artillery fire and the worst battlefield conditions known to man were in effect. The entire salient became a sea of oozing, yellow mud at depths which slowed movement to a crawl and, at worst, drowned men. The thousands of rotting corpses littering the battlefield accentuated the horror.

Movement could only take place at night, out of sight of the German artillery, on wooden tracks called bath mats, laid and continuously maintained by soldiers and pioneers. Off the tracks, the men could barely move. The Germans, aware of this position, shelled the tracks intermittently, killing men and horses transporting munitions and supplies to the front.

The Canadian troops launched their attacks close to dawn following a protective barrage. Soldiers, heavily laden with rifles, ammunition, shovels and other accoutrements of war rose from their shell holes or ditch-like trenches and moved sluggishly toward the Germans. Slowed by mud often nearly one metre deep, they often lost the coverage of their barrage and fell victim to German counter-battery and machine-gun fire. The wounded departed quickly from the action, but many of those immobilized by their injuries drowned in the merciless mud.

Exacerbating the difficulties at Passchendaele, six of the Canadian battalions wore kilts into battle. The heavy skirts became coated in mud adding extra weight and discomfort to the soldiers.

Sleep for all men in these horrific conditions, before or after an attack, was almost impossible.

As you read about this battle and the various attacks, do not forget the hardships beyond the bullets and the shells.

THE CANADIANS AT PASSCHENDAELE
October and November 1917
HISTORICAL OVERVIEW

The Canadian attacks on the Passchendaele Ridge in late October and early November of 1917 capped a major British offensive that commenced on July 31. The capture of the Bellevue Spur and the village of Passchendaele is known as the 8th battle of the Third Battle of Ypres.

The British High Command's objective in this offensive was to break through the Ypres Salient and seize the German-occupied Belgian channel ports. Unfortunately, as with most battles of the First World War, the objectives were beyond the capabilities of the strategists and the armies. British, French, New Zealand, Australian and Canadian troops were thrown against the German defenses in the most harrowing conditions with little hope of success. By the time the offensive closed down, more than 250,000 Commonwealth soldiers were dead, wounded or missing for a gain of less than seven kilometres.

The offensive began at 3:50 a.m. on July 31, 1917. Initially, British attacks radiating eastward from Ypres met with success. Troops captured Pilkem and drove northeast toward Langemarck and St. Julien, advancing more than two kilometres. Immediately, the Germans counterattacked and recaptured some of the hard-won territory. In the southern area of attack, Hooge and Bellewaerde Ridge fell, regaining ground lost in 1915 for the Allies. Nevertheless, the Germans had stymied the advance and over the next few days managed to stop the British in their tracks.

At this point the British High Command encountered a new enemy, the weather. After the initial attack, the torrential Flanders rain came down for three days and turned the low-lying region into a sea of mud. For the next two weeks, local attacks produced some gains but it was not until August 16 that the Allies renewed the assault on the old 1915 battleground. During the Battle of Langemarck, which lasted until August 18, the British successfully captured the villages of Langemarck and St. Julien. Progress was slow and although the gains were respectable, the breakthrough

The Belgian Front prior to the Third Battle of Ypres

had not been made. Between the start of the battle on July 31 and the end of August, the British army suffered 70,800 casualties.

Local actions continued through the summer, but the Germans had the advantage of the heights to observe the British movements and pour accurate artillery fire on the exposed positions.

The next major attack was launched on September 20 when the British High Command decided to exploit their successes on the Gheluvelt plateau. At 5:40 a.m. British and Australian troops attacked in the general direction of Zonnebeke. Between September 20 and 25, along ground churned into a morass by rain and incessant shellfire, the armies drove against the German positions along the Menin road. On September 26, in the Battle of Polygon Wood, Polygon Wood and Zonnebeke fell and German morale appeared to be faltering. The British and Australians suffered 35,000 casualties between September 20 and October 3.

A breakthrough seemed possible when the attack was renewed on October 4 in the Battle of Broodseinde. New Zealanders captured the Abraham Heights, Gravenstafel and Boetleer's Farm. Poelcapelle was captured by the British on the northern flank and Australian patrols entered Passchendaele village, the highest point on the ridge.

With a foothold on the ridge, the Allies could now exploit these hard-won positions. On October 9 and 12, British, Australian and New Zealand soldiers fought for the desired break through the German lines. However, the faltering German morale recovered and the Australians and New Zealanders were stopped by German wire, artillery and well-placed machine gun positions. The successes of late September and October 4 disappeared in the cruel mud of Flanders. Only in the north, where British troops captured ground east of Poelcapelle, had there been any success.

The offensive was spent, the weather was worsening and the fabled breakthrough existed on paper only. For their massive losses, the British armies had failed to reach the Passchendaele Ridge never mind the Channel ports. In spite of these conditions, the British High Command decided to continue the campaign for several nebulous reasons. This time the Canadian Corps would be fed to the mud and the guns.

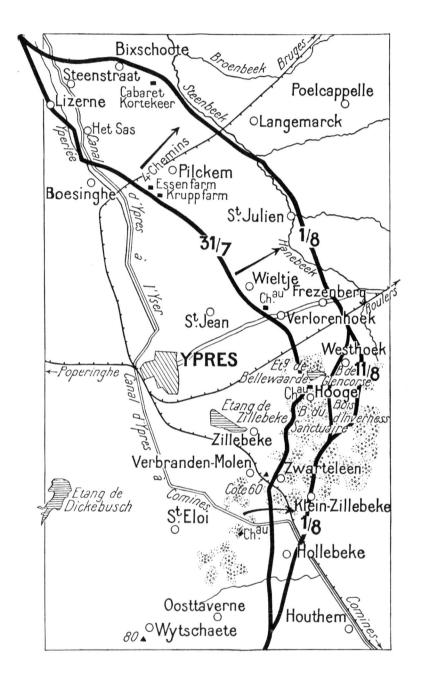

First stage of the Third Battle of Ypres, July 31 to August 11, 1917

Commanded now by a Canadian, Sir Arthur Currie, the Canadian Corps was having a successful year. Although 1917 was the bleakest year of the war for the Allies, it was one success after another for the Canadians: Vimy, Arleux, Fresnoy and Hill 70 all fell to the Corps. The Canadians had developed a reputation for success, efficiency and planning. Passchendaele would be a crushing test. Currie was reluctant to accept the Canadian role in continuing the offensive. He saw no strategic reason to expend lives in the capture of Passchendaele. His objections were overruled, but he did win a delay in starting the attack until his Canadians were completely ready.

The returning Canadians who fought at Ypres in 1915 and 1916 were shocked at the scenes in the salient. Everything had been destroyed. Nothing green remained. The dead of the earlier battles were everywhere and the ground was a maze of interconnected, water-filled shell holes. The air was full of the stench of decomposing bodies.

The Canadian plan was simple. They would attack in a series of battles, each with a limited objective. Step by step, they would take the village. But before they could start, the transport system, the artillery and communications had to be in place. On October 17, Canadian engineers and pioneers began to extend the transport system, construct artillery positions and move ammunition and supplies to the front. The work continued in the face of continuous enemy shelling, including the deadly gas shells. By October 26, they were ready to go over the top.

The overall objective of the Canadian attack was to secure a defensible position on the Passchendaele Ridge. If successful, they would drive a thin wedge into the German positions, leaving them exposed to enemy fire from all directions. As the front of the Canadian Corps was split in two by the impassable morass that had been the valley of the Ravebeek River, their only option was to launch a two-pronged offensive up the drier spurs of the ridge. The 3rd Canadian Division was to attack the Bellevue Spur and advance 1,200 metres toward Passchendaele. The 58th Battalion (Central Ontario) would attack along the Gravenstafel-Passchendaele road with the 43rd Battalion (Cameron Highlanders of Winnipeg) and the 52nd Battalion (Lake Superior) on their left. The 4th Canadian

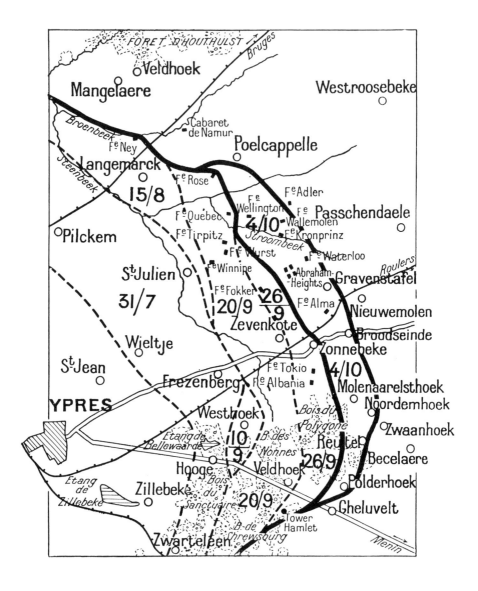

Advance in the Third Battle of Ypres to October 4, 1917

Mounted Rifles would be on the Corps' northern flank. South of the morass of the Ravebeek, the 4th Canadian Division would attack up the Passchendaele Ridge using the 46th (South Saskatchewan). The 47th (British Columbia) and the 44th (Manitoba) Battalions would follow up the assault of the 46th.

The attack went in at 5:40 a.m. on October 26. The 58th and 43rd Battalions of the 3rd Division advanced along the Gravenstafel-Passchendaele road and captured the German positions. But shelling turned them back. Throughout the Battle at Passchendaele, individual feats of bravery saved situations that appeared lost. A group of the 43rd Battalion held onto its valuable position on the Bellevue Spur, thus enabling reinforcements to arrive to save the Canadian gains. Lieutenant Robert Shankland won the Victoria Cross for his courage on the Bellevue Spur that day.

Similar feats of bravery enabled both the 52nd and 4th Canadian Mounted Rifles Battalions to achieve and defend gains against horrendous odds. Following Shankland's advance, Major C. P. J. O'Kelly, MC, led his company of the 52nd and advanced Canadian positions by capturing 100 prisoners and destroying six pillboxes. Private Tommy Holmes of the 4th Canadian Mounted Rifles had similarly saved a desperate situation. When his unit was pinned down by heavy German machine gun fire, Holmes singlehandedly knocked out two machine guns and captured a pillbox and 19 German prisoners, opening the way for the 4th Canadian Mounted Rifles to advance. Both O'Kelly and Holmes were awarded the Victoria Cross.

Even with these feats of bravery, the 3rd Division was unable to achieve its limited objective that day. Yet at Passchendaele, any gains were good. They dug in and prepared for the next phase.

On the south, the 46th Battalion's attack was successful and the follow-up attacks by the 47th and 44th Battalions on October 27 moved the line 700 metres closer to Passchendaele.

The next phase of the attack took place on October 30, a continuation of the October 26 advance.

The 3rd Division would continue its assault toward Passchendaele. This time the Princess Patricia's Canadian Light Infantry (PPCLI) would attack into the valley of the Ravebeek, the

49th (Edmonton) would take the north side of the Gravenstafel-Passchendaele road and, north of them, the 5th Canadian Mounted Rifles (Quebec) would secure the northern flank of the attack.

The 4th Division was south on the Passchendaele Ridge. The 85th (Nova Scotia Highlanders) was to attack south of the Passchendaele-Zonnebeke road, the 78th (Winnipeg Grenadiers) across the Passchendaele-Zonnebeke road and the 72nd (Seaforth Highlanders of Vancouver) north of the road initially and then turn north to capture the German defenses at Crest Farm, west of Passchendaele village.

They attacked at 5:50 a.m. on October 30. Initially, all went well; however, heavy German opposition and artillery fire crushed the attacks of the PPCLI and the 49th Battalion. Only individual acts of courage brought a measure of success to the attack. When a major German pillbox on the Gravenstafel-Passchendaele road held up the 3rd Division's attack, Lieutenant Hugh McKenzie, DCM, of the 7th Machine Guns company led a frontal attack on the position while a second group under Sergeant G. H. Mullin, MM, of the PPCLI outflanked and captured the pillbox. McKenzie was killed during the frontal attack. Both men were awarded the Victoria Cross. The PPCLI and the 49th suffered heavy losses for gains of about 500 metres.

On the northern flank, the 5th Canadian Mounted Rifles led by Major George Pearkes performed the most courageous act of the battle and, in no small way, ensured the capture of Passchendaele. Pearkes was concerned that the British units would be unable to keep up with the Canadian advance, so he allocated a group of the 5th Canadian Mounted Rifles to capture Source Farm which was in the British sphere of operation.

Advancing against heavy machine gun fire and across open ground, the 5th Canadian Mounted Rifles attacked in small groups and successfully captured and held the major German defences at Source and Vapour Farms. It seems incomprehensible how these small groups held out against the Germans under these circumstances. Undoubtedly, this action saved the Canadian attack of October 30 and ensured the capture of the village in future operations. It was one of the bravest small-group actions by Canadians in

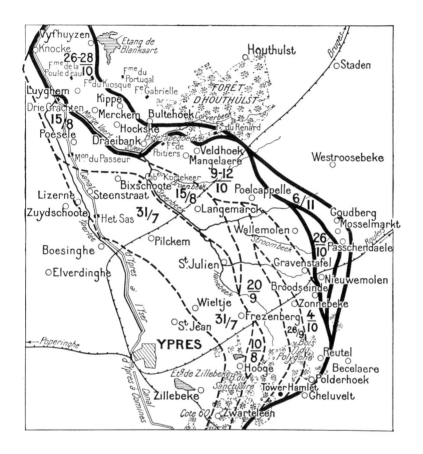

The Sixth and final stage of the Third Battle of Ypres - November 6, 1917

the entire war. Pearkes was awarded the Victoria Cross for leading this attack.

Similar to October 26, the 3rd Division was short of its objective and paid a very heavy price for these gains. The 4th Division attack on the Passchendaele Ridge went according to plan. Although suffering heavy casualties, the 85th Battalion had advanced and captured Vienna Cottages. The 78th had succeeded on their flank and the 72nd completed its difficult attack and captured Crest Farm.

The Canadians were now well up on the ridge, on drier land, so that when the assault was renewed by the 1st and 2nd Divisions on November 6, the remains of the village of Passchendaele were within grasp.

The 1st Division attacked at 6:00 a.m. The 1st (Western Ontario) and 2nd (Eastern Ontario) Battalions captured Mosselmarkt and the ridge north of the village. The 3rd Battalion (Toronto Regiment) protected the northern flank by capturing Vine Cottages. Private C. F. Barron of the 3rd Battalion captured three enemy machine gun posts enabling his battalion to secure its position. He was awarded the Victoria Cross. The attack launched from the drier ground was a success.

The 2nd Division, using the 27th Battalion (City of Winnipeg), attacked and captured the remains of Passchendaele, while the 31st (Alberta) and the 28th (Saskatchewan) Battalions charged out of the Ravebeek Valley to capture the ridge north of the village. Private J. P. Robertson of the 27th destroyed an important German machine gun post, opening the way for the attack. Robertson, who was later killed, was awarded the Victoria Cross posthumously.

The Canadians were now firmly established on top of the Passchendaele Ridge. On November 10, the final Canadian attack was launched to secure the position on the ridge. North of the village, the 7th (British Columbia) and the 8th (Black Devils of Winnipeg) Battalions successfully captured Valour Farm and Vindictive Crossroads. On their southern flank, the 20th Battalion (Central Ontario) of the 2nd Division also succeeded in pushing the Germans down the eastern side of the ridge.

The view of rolling green countryside to the east must have seemed like heaven to the advancing troops, for the view westward toward Ypres was that of hell. The Third Battle of Ypres ended with the attack of November 10. It had cost the Commonwealth more than 250,000 dead, wounded and missing. The price the Canadians paid for their two-week tenure at Passchendaele was more than 5,000 lives. All told, 16,000 were killed, wounded and missing.

The Canadians held the line at Passchendaele until mid-November when they were withdrawn to the Vimy-Lens sector. It was their last visit to the immortal Ypres Salient. They had fought here in 1915 at Second Ypres, 1916 at Mount Sorrel and now at Passchendaele. They had left more than 15,000 of their comrades in the soil of Flanders.

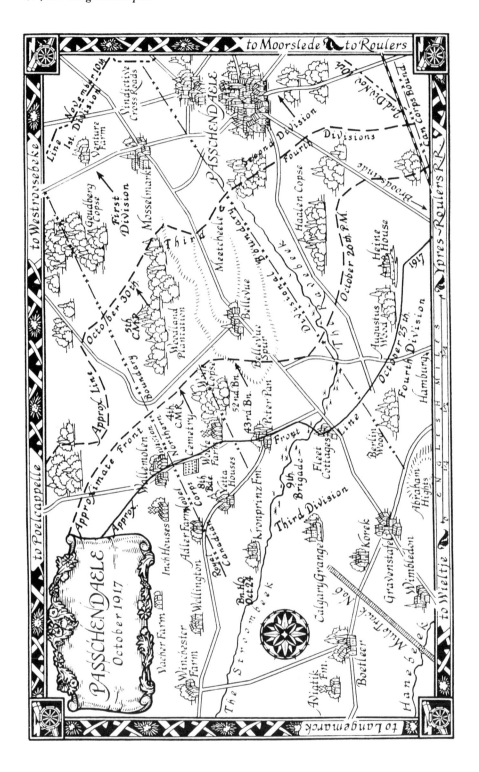

TOUR ITINERARY:
Duration 5 Hours

THE BATTLE OF PASSCHENDAELE —
October to November, 1917

Point 1:   *Jump off, October 26, 1917, Wolf Farm and Marsh Bottom.*

Point 2:   *The attack of October 30, 1917, Source Farm*

Point 3:   *The attack of October 30, 1917, Meetcheele*

Point 4:   *The attack of November 6, 1917, Passchendaele New British Cemetery*

Point 5:   *The attack of November 10, 1917, Vindictive Crossroads*

Point 6:   *Crest Farm*

Point 7:   *The attack of the 4th Division, October 30, 1917, the 85th Nova Scotia Highlanders Memorial*

Point 8:   *The Valley of the Ravebeek, Tyne Cot Cemetery*

THE BATTLE OF PASSCHENDAELE

THE TOUR

You will notice some difference in spelling of place names. The names used during the First World War were French, whereas today the road signs are written in Flemish. Please refer to the list at the beginning of this book. In my text, I have used the French spellings from 1915.

The tour begins in the Grote Markt in Ypres. Follow the one-way system of the Grote Markt, exiting toward the northeast left of the hotel de ville. Follow the signs to Poelcappelle and Roulers. You will pass through St. Jean and Wieltje.

During the First World War, this road was essential to the Allies and was under observation by the German artillery. Nothing moved along this road during the day, but at night it became a hive of activity.

After you have passed through Wieltje, turn right at the junction and follow the road to Poelcapelle and Roulers.

This territory was severely contested in April 1915. Canadian, British and Indian soldiers attacked the German flank north of this road in an effort to close a huge gap created by the first use of poison gas.

Continue through the village of St. Julien, the scene of heavy fighting for the Canadians April 24 and 25, 1915, toward the hamlet of Keerselaere. The Canadian monument, erected in honor of the Canadians' Second Battle of Ypres, is on your right. Turn right in front of the memorial onto the Gravenstafel road and follow the first small road on your left toward the windmill for 2.25 kilometres until you reach the high point.

This is the Gravenstafel Ridge, the critical defensive position held by the Canadians in April 1915.[1] The view from here is excellent. To the east you can see Passchendaele church, Tyne Cot British Cemetery and the large chimneys of the Zonnebeke brickyard. To the north is the Poelcapelle church and to the west the windmill and Langemarck. Ypres and the Monts des Flandres are visible to the southwest.

---

[1] See Volume I of King & Empire The Canadians at Ypres

The Passchendaele Battlefield October - November 1917

(PUBLIC ARCHIVES OF CANADA - C31652)

Continue as far as the Gravenstafel crossroads. The rise ahead, just past the crossroads on the right, was known as The Abraham Heights. This is from where the Canadian reserve and support troops moved to the front. It was shelled severely throughout the battle. Turn left after the New Zealand memorial (Battle of Broodseinde, October 4, 1917). Continue along the Passchendaele road, out of the hamlet and past a calvary on your left. The road dips and crosses a small creek, the Ravebeek (it is signposted). The area to the north and south was known as Marsh Bottom. The Canadian jump-off line was 250 metres east of the Ravebeek Creek. The high ground of the Passchendaele Ridge is across the valley.

After you cross the creek, turn left on Ravestraat. Continue up Ravestraat for 500 metres until the road veers to the left. The farm on your left was known as Peter Pan in 1917. Keep right and follow the road for 250 metres until you arrive at a farm.

Point 1: Jump off, October 26, 1917, Wolf Farm and Marsh Bottom.

The Canadians' strategy at the Battle of Passchendaele was to launch a series of limited attacks designed to attain the heights of the ridge. Each attack was a two-pronged affair separated by the marshy, impassable valley of the Ravebeek. The 3rd and, later, the 1st Canadian Divisions attacked along the Bellevue Spur that is the height directly east of you where you were just driving. The spur joins the Passchendaele Ridge north of the village. The attack by the 4th and, later, 2nd Canadian Divisions took place across the valley of the Ravebeek on the Passchendaele Ridge.

You are standing at the jump-off line for the attack by the 3rd Canadian Division on October 26, 1917. From here you can see Tyne Cot Cemetery and Passchendaele church and the rise of the Bellevue Spur east of you. The objective was to secure positions 1,200 metres on drier ground up the ridge. The attack was set as follows: the 58th Battalion would attack south of the Passchendaele road, the 43rd Camerons north of the road, the 52nd Battalion to its left and the 4th Canadian Mounted Rifles (Central Ontario)[2] would hold the left flank. You are standing in the center of the 4th

---

[2] This title is misleading as the four Mounted Rifle Battalions serving were infantry. None of them ever used a horse in battle.

Canadian Mounted Rifles' line. Wolf Farm, 100 metres east of you, and Wolf Copse, directly east of it, were the objectives.

Launching the attack at 5:40 a.m., the 43rd and 58th Battalions successfully captured Bellevue (the small number of buildings on the Passchendaele Road east of you) and pushed forward. The German artillery at the observation posts on the ridge reacted quickly. Shells rained down on the attackers and the Canadians began to pull back.

The attack by the 58th Battalion south of the road into the Ravebeek Valley met stiff resistance and heavy artillery fire. They were halted after gaining 400 to 500 metres of ground.

North of the road, the 43rd Battalion captured a small portion of land on the higher levels of the spur, but their advance was stopped by machine gun and artillery fire. A platoon under the command of Lieutenant Robert Shankland successfully defended the gains against several counterattacks. Only 700 metres from their jump-off point, the small band refused to give up their toehold. Shankland returned to the front lines to get help and then bravely crossed No Man's Land to rejoin his men. A company of the 52nd Battalion under Captain Christopher O'Kelly came to support the endangered position and the Canadians were able to preserve their meager gains. Both O'Kelly[3] and Shankland[4] were awarded the Victoria Cross.[5]

The 4th Canadian Mounted Rifles attacked and were immediately pinned down at the point where you now stand. When all seemed lost on the facing slopes, Private Tommy Holmes ran across No Man's Land, from shell hole to shell hole, and singlehandedly destroyed two German machine-gun positions and a pillbox. His actions saved the Rifles from annihilation and permitted the attack to continue. Miraculously, Holmes survived!

---

[3] Captain Christopher Patrick John O'Kelly, VC, MC, was born in Winnipeg, Manitoba on November 18, 1895 and died at Lac Seal, Ontario on November 15, 1922.

[4] Lieutenant Robert Shankland, VC, DCM, was born at Ayr, Scotland on October 10, 1897 and died in Vancouver on January 20, 1968.

[5] Three men who lived on the same street in Winnipeg, R. W. Hall, Leo Clarke and Shankland, won the Victoria Cross in the Great War. Hall won his VC posthumously at Second Ypres April 24, 1915 and Clarke won his in September 1916 near Pozieres on the Somme. He died of wounds October 1916.

Canadian Pioneers laying trench mats, November 1917

For his bravery, the 19-year-old Holmes was awarded the Victoria Cross.[6]

Although these acts of bravery had advanced the Canadian front only 400 to 700 metres toward the drier ground of the Bellevue Spur, it was considered a success by Passchendaele standards. The Canadians consolidated and fought off German counterattacks. The 4th Division's attack on the Passchendaele Ridge had also advanced the line. Slowly, the creeping, bloody approach to Passchendaele was being secured.

Return to the Passchendaele road and turn left past the small collection of buildings that is Bellevue. You are crossing the area won by the Canadians on October 26, 1917. After 900 metres, beyond the buildings at Bellevue, you come to a crossroads. Turn left and continue for 800 metres. The jump-off line for the next

---

[6] Private Thomas William Holmes, VC, was born in Montreal on October 14, 1898 and died January 4, 1950 at Toronto.

assault, on October 30, was west of this road. Again, it was the 3rd Division that attacked along the Bellevue Spur. The 4th Division would renew its attack on the Passchendaele Ridge also. Continue 400 metres along the right fork until the road forks again. Stop at this point.

Point 2: The attack of October 30, 1917, Source Farm

The plan for October 30 was similar to that of the 26th. The 3rd Division would again assault the Bellevue Spur, with the Princess Patricia's Canadian Light Infantry (PPCLI) attacking south of the road, the 49th Battalion (Edmonton) taking the north side of the road and the 5th Canadian Mounted Rifles (Eastern Townships) attacking further north in the mush.

The farm just south of you is Source Farm. The farms to the east, left to right, are Vapour Farm, Vegetable House and Vine Cottages. The land to the south and west was a swampy morass known as Woodland Plantation. It was here on October 30 that the 5th Canadian Mounted Rifles, under Major George Pearkes, saved the Passchendaele Battle and the lives of many Canadians.

In the early morning light, at 5:50 a.m., in nightmarish conditions, the 5th Canadian Mounted Rifles pushed off from west of the road across the muddy, shell-scarred lunar landscape. From their left flank, where a British attack had failed, machine-gun fire immediately inflicted heavy casualties, threatening the entire assault.

Although it was in the British area of attack, Pearkes dispatched a small unit to capture the problem location at Source Farm. The unit, under Lieutenant Allen Otty, captured and held Source Farm until relieved. Otty was killed in the action, close to where you now stand. With the flank secure, Pearkes pushed forward to capture Vapour Farm (due east). Against heavy odds, they held these positions until relieved by the 2nd Canadian Mounted Rifles (British Columbia). They had advanced 1,000 metres and saved the Canadian flank, ensuring a good position for subsequent attacks in the forthcoming days. It was truly a remarkable achievement. The entire action took place within 300 metres of where you stand and

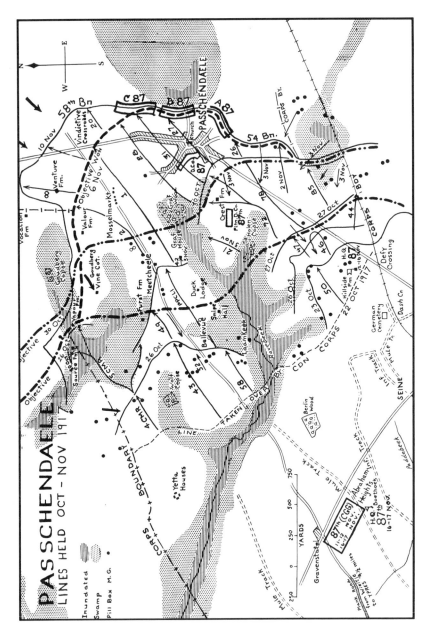

Passchendaele 1917, stages of the Canadian attack

(CANADIAN GRENADIER GUARDS)

Pearkes[7] was awarded the Victoria Cross for his role. The other attacking units of the 3rd Division had been crushed.

Return to the Passchendaele road and turn left toward Passchendaele. Stop after 450 metres.

Point 3: The attack of October 30, 1917, Meetcheele

Throughout the Battle of Passchendaele, individual exploits of heroism resulted in the successes thus far achieved by the Canadian Corps. The actions of men like Holmes and Pearkes had determined the outcome of the battle. Equally significant were the attacks of the PPCLI and the 49th Battalion.

To your right are a few small farms in the Ravebeek Valley. Pastoral now. Deadly then. Their names — Snipe Hall, Duck Lodge and Graf House — spelled death in 1917. These farms were rebuilt in the 1920s in approximately the same locations as the farms in 1917. Then, the Germans fortified the remnants and built a series of pillboxes nearby to provide cover fire. Each pillbox would have to be taken one by one in a co-ordinated, small unit action. A pillbox on the Passchendaele road at Meetcheele, where you now stand, covered all approaches with deadly fire.

After a heavy barrage, the units attacked at 5:50 a.m. and immediately encountered problems. The PPCLI to the south advanced to Duck Lodge but not without casualties to all its officers including Talbot Papineau, who was killed by the German counter barrage at the jump-off line. They captured Duck Lodge but were then pinned down by machine-gun fire from the German bunker on the Passchendaele road at Meetcheele.

Lieutenant Hugh McKenzie, realizing the situation, devised an operation to eliminate the pillbox by flanking it. McKenzie, of the 7th Company Canadian Machine Gun Corps, led the diversionary frontal attack himself. Sergeant George Mullin of the PPCLI led the enveloping action and personally captured the pillbox and its garrison.

---

[7] Lieutenant Colonel George Randolph Pearkes, VC, CB, DSO, MC, was born at Watford, England on February 26, 1888 and died in Victoria on May 30, 1984. He was the Minister of National Defence from 1957 to 1960.

STANLEY RICHARD SHORE

PRIVATE, *27th Battalion, C.E.F.*

Was born in Manitou, Manitoba, on December 16th, 1896. He received his education in the Brandon Schools and in the King Edward School, Saskatoon, Saskatchewan. He was employed by the National Trust Company, Saskatoon, for a short period, but in order to complete his education he resigned and returned to school. In October, 1915, at the age of eighteen he entered the service of the Bank of British North America in Saskatoon. Previous to his enlisting for overseas service he was attached to the 105th Regiment. He enlisted in April, 1916, as a Private in the 183rd Battalion, Canadian Infantry, and proceeded overseas. On the 183rd Battalion being disbanded in England he proceeded to France with a reinforcement draft for the 27th Battalion, Canadian Infantry. He was killed during the attack on Passchendaele Ridge on November 6th, 1917.

WILLIAM ARNOLD PALMER

LIEUTENANT, *43rd Battalion, C.E.F.*

Was born in Snettisham, England, in October, 1887, a son of the Rev. F. W. H. Palmer. After completing his education at the Grammar School, Snettisham, he entered the service of Lloyds Bank, Limited, where he remained for nine years. He then came to Canada and joined the staff of the Bank of Montreal in Winnipeg, in 1913. In March, 1915, he enlisted as a Private in the 43rd Battalion, Canadian Infantry, and arrived in France with his unit in the following summer. In July, 1916, during the heavy fighting on the Somme, he was severely wounded at Courcelette, and evacuated to England. On his recovery he was given his commission as Lieutenant, and he rejoined his former battalion in the field in July, 1917. He was instantly killed on November 14th, 1917, while leading his platoon forward during the operations against Passchendaele.

Bellevue Pillbox, 1919

McKenzie[9] was killed in the frontal attack and his body was never recovered. Both he and Mullin[10] were awarded the Victoria Cross for bravery.

On the north side of the road, the 49th Edmontons suffered as severely as the PPCLI. Their attack was halted by the German barrage. Roughly 100 metres north of you, Private Cecil "Hoodoo" Kinross of the 49th singlehandedly attacked a main German machine-gun position and killed the crew. For his bravery, which saved the 49th attack from complete disaster, Kinross[11] was awarded the Victoria Cross.

At the end of the day, the 49th Battalion and PPCLI had advanced only 300 to 600 metres along the front for 443 and 363

---

[9] Lieutenant Hugh McKenzie, VC, DCM, was born at Liverpool, England on December 5, 1885.
[10] Sergeant George Harry Mullin, VC, was born in Portland, Oregon on August 15, 1892 and died in Regina on April 5, 1963.
[11] Private Cecil John Kinross, VC, was born at Clackmannan, Scotland on July 13, 1897 and died at Lougheed, Alberta on June 21, 1957.

TALBOT PAPINEAU

Born into a privileged and famous family at Montebello, Quebec on March 25, 1883, Talbot Mercer Papineau was undoubtedly destined for a distinguished political career. His unfortunate fate, however, was a premature and altogether undistinguished end in the mud of Passchendaele, a victim of his own father's generation.

He was the son of Louis-Joseph Papineau and Caroline Rogers of Philadelphia, and the grandson of Louis-Joseph Papineau, leader of the famed Lower Canada Rebellion of 1837. A product of two cultures, Papineau became the perfect anglicized French Canadian. Educated at McGill and later, as a Rhodes Scholar, at Oxford, he was typical of the Canadian elite of the era.

He set himself up for a political career by starting his own law practice in Montreal where his family and social connections quickly aided his ambitions. Politically, Papineau's views were modern, more those of a Canadian Nationalist than a supporter of the Empire. His family's wealth allowed him the freedom to do as he pleased and hard work was unlikely required to help him along his chosen path.

With the declaration of war in August 1914, the 31-year-old bachelor rushed to join the privately-raised Princess Patricia's Canadian Light Infantry (PPCLI), a regiment financed by his good friend Hamilton Gault of Montreal. Papineau easily received a commission and served with the PPCLI in France beginning in February 1915.

He was awarded the Military Cross for bravery during a trench raid at St. Eloi, Belgium on February 27 and survived the grim battle at Bellewaerde Ridge on May 8, where the PPCLI suffered 397 casualties.

Then, in late 1915, suffering from "battle fatigue," Papineau was invalided to a hospital on the coast of France. In February 1916, he took a staff appointment behind the lines. Always conscious of appearances, he knew he was helping his career in many ways, but did not like the fact many of his fellow officers would see him as "windy."

Safe behind the front, Papineau witnessed the fates of his comrades through the 1916 battles of Mount Sorrel and the Somme, where the PPCLI suffered heavily. At this point, Papineau was heavily involved in the public debate over the role of French Canada in the war. But he knew it was easy to talk about sacrifice when you are a long way from the fighting.

In 1917, his old regiment was successful in the capture of Vimy Ridge on April 9. This was a great day for Canada, and Papineau, once again, was aware of his distance from the action. Mindful of how this might hurt his future political ambitions, he finally decided to return to the Patricias in May.

At 5:50 a.m. on October 30, 1917, the Canadians attacked and, minutes later, Papineau was instantly killed by a direct hit from a German shell. His last words were, "Hughie[8], this is suicide." Papineau may be remembered for fighting in the PPCLI's worst battle of the war. The regiment suffered 363 killed, wounded and missing for an insignificant advance against the Germans. There was no time to bury the dead and Papineau was among the many left unburied. A couple of weeks later, a PPCLI party found "a pair of feet with reversed putties . . . sticking out of a shell hole full of water . . .

"Major Papineau always wore his putties that way. They pulled the body out and, by examining the contents of the pockets, found it to be Papineau. Part of a shell had hit him in the stomach blowing everything else above away, poor fellow. He could not have known what hit him."

A cross was placed over the remains but in 1919, when the battlefields were cleared, only the cross was found.

Talbot Papineau, with all his hopes and dreams, is commemorated by name only on the Menin Gate Memorial in Ypres.

---

[8] H. W. Niven, DSO and bar, MC, Adjutant of the PPCLI.

casualties respectively. Although the attack of October 30 had not reached its full objectives, it had inched the Canadians, once again, closer to the prize of Passchendaele village. The costs of such gains and for such a prize must, however, be questioned. How did any of these men, fighting in these conditions under shellfire, machine gun bullets and counterattacks, survive?

The next stage occurred seven days later.

Return to your car and continue 400 metres to Passchendaele New British Cemetery.

Point 4: The attack of November 6, 1917, Passchendaele New British Cemetery

Before discussing the attack of November 6, I would like you to walk to the back of the cemetery from where you can view, to the northwest, the area to which the 5th Canadian Mounted Rifles advanced on October 30. Return to the entrance of the cemetery, which overlooks the village of Passchendaele.

Across the Ravebeek Valley is the Canadian memorial park, built on the grounds of Crest Farm, which was captured after severe fighting by the 72nd Seaforth Highlanders of Vancouver. Notice the short distances involved here and contemplate the plan for the November 6 capture of Passchendaele and the area north. Although the October 30 assault did not achieve all its objectives, roughly 800 metres up the Bellevue Spur were gained. It was the 1st and 2nd Divisions, relieving the depleted 3rd and 4th Divisions, who launched the attack of November 6. The 1st Division was to attack up the Bellevue Spur and onto the Passchendaele Ridge north of the village. The 1st Battalion (Western Ontario) would advance south of the Passchendaele road and capture Mosselmarkt. The 2nd Battalion (Eastern Ontario) was to attack north of the road.

The knowledge gained through earlier operations on how effectively to eliminate the German pillbox positions was effectively carried out. The attack, which commenced at 6:00 a.m., succeeded in its objectives, capturing the land to your left up the Passchendaele road approximately 1.4 kilometres from the jump-off line which was 500 metres east of you. On the left flank of the 1st Division's attack, the 3rd Battalion (Toronto Regiment) launched

View of Passchendaele village from Passchendaele New British Cemetery (Bellevue Spur)

(N. CHRISTIE)

View across the valley of the Paddebek toward Crest Farm from Passchendaele New British Cemetery (Bellevue Spur)

(N. CHRISTIE)

Meetcheele Pillbox, looking towards Gravenstafel, 1919
(PUBLIC ARCHIVES OF CANADA - PA 4559)

a subsidiary assault on Vine Cottages, the remaining German stronghold after the October 30 battle. The 3rd Battalion was pinned down from the outset and, again, heroic acts by individual soldiers revived the attack.

At Vine Cottages, the farm 400 metres to the northwest, Corporal Colin Barron[12] of the 3rd Battalion singlehandedly destroyed a German machine-gun position and killed the crew, which allowed the attack to progress. The 3rd Battalion captured the farm by midmorning. This action is best viewed from the back of the cemetery.

The southern attack, launched simultaneously by the 2nd Division, matched the success of the 1st Division. Passchendaele village fell. Across the valley is the Crest Farm Canadian battlefield memorial. It was from near that point that the 28th (Saskatchewan), 31st (Alberta) and 27th (City of Winnipeg) Battalions launched

---

[12] Corporal Colin Fraser Barron, VC, was born at Banff on September 20, 1893 and died in Toronto, August 15, 1958.

HOW IT REALLY WAS

The battlefield of Passchendaele is beyond modern understanding. Even if you go back through contemporary literature, soldier authors seem to be unable to communicate the true horrors of the battlefield.

The description below is from the First World War classic, "The Great War As I Saw It" by Canon Frederick Scott, the padre of the First Canadian Division. He missed the battle and was moving up the line to find his unit.

"Then I started to walk up the terrible, muddy roads till I came to the different German pill-boxes which had been converted into headquarters for the battalions. Finally, after wading through water and mud nearly up to my knees, I found myself the next afternoon wandering near Goudberg Copse, with a clear view of the ruins of Passchendaele, which was held by another division on our right. The whole region was unspeakably horrible. Rain was falling, the dreary waste of shell-ploughed mud, yellow and clinging, stretched off into the distance as far as the eye could see. Bearer parties, tired and pale, were carrying out the wounded on stretchers, making a journey of several miles in doing so. The bodies of dead men lay here and there where they had fallen in the advance. I came across one poor boy who had been killed that morning. His body was covered with a shiny coating of yellow mud, and looked like a statue made of bronze. He had a beautiful face, with finely shaped head covered with close, curling hair, and looked more like some work of art than a human being. The huge shell holes were half full of water often reddened with human blood, and many of the wounded had rolled down in the pools and been drowned. As I went on, someone I met told me that there was a wounded man in the trenches ahead of me.

"I made my way in the direction indicated and shouted out asking if anybody was there. Suddenly I heard a faint voice replying, and I hurried to the place from which the sound came. There I found sitting up in the mud of the trench, his legs almost covered with water, a lad who told me that he had been there for many hours. I never saw anything like the wonderful expression on his face. He was smiling most cheerfully, and made no complaint about what he had suffered. I told him I would get a stretcher, so I went to some trenches not far away and got a bearer party and a stretcher and went over to rescue him. The men jumped down into the trench and moved him very gently, but his legs were so numb that although they were hit he felt no pain. One of the men asked him if he was hit in the legs. He said, "Yes," but the man looked up at me and pulling up the boy's tunic showed me a hideous wound in his back."

the attack on the village. After fierce hand-to-hand fighting in the heap of rubble that was Passchendaele, the village was successfully in Canadian hands. The 2nd Division swept through the village to the Passchendaele-Westrosebeek road and joined hands with the 1st Division north of the village. After 11 days of hard fighting, the Canadians were on top of the Passchendaele Ridge. There would be another effort to secure their territory on November 10.

Return to your car and continue along the Passchendaele road. You will pass through the territory captured by the 1st Canadian Division on November 6. After 800 metres you come to the Passchendaele/Westrosebeek crossroads, once known as Vindictive Crossroads. Stop across the road.

Point 5: The attack of November 10, 1917, Vindictive Crossroads

From this point, appreciating the tactical importance of Passchendaele Ridge is easy. To the south, you can see the village and perhaps grasp the power of the whole ridge. You have a good view of the successful attack of the 27th Battalion on Passchendaele. The attack of November 10 was intended to secure the high ground around the village and improve the salient created by the Canadian attacks.

The principal units used in the attack were the 7th (British Columbia), the 8th (Winnipeg Rifles) and the 20th (Central Ontario) Battalions from the 2nd Division. The objectives of the 7th and 8th Battalions were Hill 62 on the Goudeberg Spur northwest of the Passchendaele-Westrosebeek road, and the edge of the ridge north and east of Vindictive Crossroads. Venture Farm, the farm west of where you stand, was a strong German defensive position. Its capture was the responsibility of the 8th Battalion.

The attack commenced at 6:00 a.m. and, except for minor problems on the left flank, all objectives were secured by early morning. Look east to see the edge of the ridge captured and the green fields further east, which must have appeared like a paradise to Canadian soldiers that November day. This was the end of the Passchendaele Battle for the Canadians. Several battalions had additional tours in front lines, but the heavy fighting was over. The Canadian Corps was withdrawn during the third week of November, never to return to the Ypres Salient.

Although they had achieved their goal, they had driven a narrow and extremely vulnerable wedge into German-held territory.[13]

Return to your car and follow the road into Passchendaele. As you enter the village, you will pass the territory captured by the Canadians on November 6. Turn right at the church and follow the signs to the Canadian battlefield memorial at Crest Farm.

Point 6 - Crest Farm

Look north from here to the Bellevue Spur and Passchendaele New British Cemetery. If you look east and west (Ypres is visible in the west) you will more easily comprehend the importance of this ridge to the Germans.

Although trees block much of the view, this was the area fought for and won by the 72nd Battalion on October 30, 1917 in a brilliant flanking operation. This action ranks in importance with the capture of Source and Vapour Farms by the 5th Canadian Mounted Rifles.

Notice how close the village is to Crest Farm, keeping in mind that a second major attack (November 6) was required to take that final stride. It is from this region that the 2nd Division launched its attack of November 6. The 27th Battalion captured the village, but a German machine-gun emplacement held up the unit until personal bravery broke the defenses. Private James Robertson of the 27th led a one-man attack across open ground on the German position and killed part of the crew while the rest fled. Robertson,[14] who earned the Victoria Cross for his heroism, was killed later in the day. He is buried in Tyne Cot Military Cemetery.

The 28th Battalion and the 31st Battalion attacked on your left, pulling out of the Ravebeek Valley to capture German positions on the ridge. The battalions then battled on into the ruined village and finally captured this long-sought prize.

Follow the road to your right as far as the turning circle. It is within walking distance.

From this position, the view to Bellevue Spur and the valley of the Ravebeek is excellent. In 1917, it was all a deadly morass. Look

---

[13] Sadly, Passchendaele was evacuated without a fight during the German offensives of 1918.
[14] Private James Peter Robertson, VC, was born at Picton, Nova Scotia on October 26, 1883.

CREST FARM CANADIAN MEMORIAL

The Canadian monument at Crest Farm, west of the village of Passchendaele, stands on one of eight First World War Canadian battlefields officially commemorated.

In 1920, the Canadian Battlefield Monument Commission decided to erect memorials at:

St. Julien - to commemorate the Second Battle of Ypres

Hill 62 - to commemorate the Battle of Mount Sorrel

Courcelette - to commemorate the Battle of the Somme

Vimy - to commemorate the Battle of Vimy Ridge

Passchendaele - to commemorate the Battle of Passchendaele

Le Quesnel - to commemorate the Battle of Amiens

Dury - to commemorate the Battle of Arras 1918 and the capture of the Drocourt-Queant line

Bourlon Wood - to commemorate the Battles of the Canal du Nord,Cambrai, the capture of Valenciennes and Mons and the March to the Rhine

It was decided that Vimy would act as the National Memorial and have a unique design. The other seven would be marked with identical memorials. A competition was held to choose an architect to design the monuments. Walter Allward of Toronto was chosen for Vimy's unique memorial and Frederick C. Clemesha of Regina took second place. Clemesha's design, "The Brooding Soldier," was built at St. Julien and had such a stark effect at its unveiling in 1923 that the Monument Commission decided it also should remain unique.

In conjunction with the architectural advisor, P. E. Nobbs, the cube design was developed for the remaining six monuments. A 13-tonne block of Stanstead granite was used for each. A wreath was carved into two sides of the monument and on the other two sides was engraved a brief explanation of the exploits of the Canadian Corps in that specific battle. One side is in English, the other in French.

At Crest Farm, the monument reads:

THE CANADIAN CORPS IN OCT. - NOV. 1917 ADVANCED ACROSS THIS VALLEY - THEN A DEADLY MORASS - CAPTURED AND HELD THE PASSCHENDAELE RIDGE

Around the base of the stone, it reads:

HONOUR TO CANADIANS WHO ON THE FIELDS OF FLANDERS AND OF FRANCE FOUGHT IN THE CAUSE OF THE ALLIES WITH SACRIFICE AND DEVOTION

These words hardly represent the sacrifice of the 5,000 men who died here and the suffering of thousands of others in the hell that was Passchendaele. They could hardly satisfy the mothers and wives whose loved ones vanished in this morass. But understatement was a sign of the times.

The view of Bellevue Spur from Crest Farm Canadian Memorial

(N. CHRISTIE)

toward the village for an impression of the difficulty in mounting an attack from here and how well the 31st and 28th Battalions executed their attack on November 6. It is hard to believe the small, pleasant and serene valley farms, known in 1917 as Duck Lodge, Snipe Hall and Graf House, were the scenes of death for hundreds of Canadians. The distances are also surprising. Can you imagine thousands of soldiers attacking behind heavy artillery and able to advance only a few hundred metres or, in some cases, not at all?

Return to the Passchendaele church and turn right on the main road to Zonnebeke. After 1.1 kilometres (past the exit sign for Passchendaele) slow down and watch for a small memorial in the fields on your left. The memorial to the 85th Battalion Nova Scotia Highlanders is not always signposted, so approach this point with caution. Stop and walk to the south side of the road.

Point 7: The attack of the 4th Division, October 30, 1917, the 85th Nova Scotia Highlanders Memorial

The Passchendaele Ridge at this point is much broader and allowed the Canadians to attack from drier, more favorable positions than on the Bellevue Spur.

Over by the village, you can see the terrain attacked and captured by the 4th Division on October 30. You are standing at their jump-off line. East of the small memorial in the fields, the 85th Battalion successfully attacked across the fields and captured Vienna Cottages on the eastern side of the ridge. But not without heavy losses.

North of the 85th, the 78th Battalion (Winnipeg Grenadiers) attacked across the road facing you, toward the northeast. They gained 900 metres toward their objective. On the left, the 72nd Battalion drove northeast along the inside slope of the ridge and turned north to capture Crest Farm. Its tremendous attack faced heavy enfilade fire. In the battles of October 1917, the 4th Division was considerably more successful than the 3rd Division. This is, however, a bit misleading as the Germans knew the importance of Bellevue Spur and defended that position ferociously.

Look south down the road to Zonnebeke (the chimneys are visible) at the ground captured by the 46th (Saskatchewan), 47th (British Columbia) and 44th (Manitoba) Battalions on October 26.

Walk along the grass path to the 85th Battalion memorial, which was erected by the men of the battalion to commemorate their worst losses of the war. A bronze plaque lists the names of officers and men killed or missing and presumed dead in the Passchendaele Battle. The monument is roughly where the jump-off line for the 85th Battalion was on October 30.

The 85th Nova Scotia Highlanders (4th Division) attacked east of you, due east toward Vienna Cottages Farm (which is still there), 500 metres northeast of the 85th monument. They captured the eastern side of the ridge.

The jump-off positions of the 4th Division on October 26 were some 800 metres to the west and southwest. From those positions, the 46th and 50th (Alberta) Battalions pushed up the Passchendaele Ridge about 500 to 900 metres along the front. After their attack, the 47th Battalion and 44th Battalion leapfrogged the 46th and 50th, but gains were minimal.

Decline Copse, 180 metres to the south, was captured and lost by the 46th Battalion and finally captured and held against fierce counterattacks by the 85th and 44th Battalions on October 27 and

The ruins of Passchendaele village

(NATIONAL ARCHIVES OF CANADA - PA 4557)

The view of Passchendaele village from Crest Farm Canadian Memorial

(N. CHRISTIE)

*The eastern view from the 85th Nova Scotia Highlanders Memorial
(Vienna Cottages is in the right background)*

(N. CHRISTIE)

28, 1917. The old Ypres-Roulers railway line used to run through the copse. For orientation, the chimneys of the Zonnebeke brickworks are clearly visible.

Return to your car and continue toward Zonnebeke. You will see a signpost for Tyne Cot British Cemetery after 900 metres. Turn right and follow the road to the cemetery. Just before you reach the cemetery, the road veers left. Turn right, pass the cemetery and stop at the sharp left-hand turn about 300 metres along the road.

Point 8: The Valley of the Ravebeek, Tyne Cot Cemetery

This was the jump-off position of the 46th Battalion of the 4th Division, on October 26. The view from here shows clearly the Bellevue Spur, the Ravebeek Valley and Passchendaele two kilometres distant. It cost Canada 5,000 lives and 11,000 wounded soldiers to reach that village. The 46th Battalion attacked at 5:40 a.m. and advanced 800 metres against problematic enemy machine-gun fire. Other 4th Division battalions took over the attack and pushed the line forward *(Point 7)*.

Canadian Monument, Passchendaele Ridge, by Mary Riter Hamilton.

German prisoners and Canadian wounded after the battle, November 1917

(PUBLIC ARCHIVES OF CANADA - PA 40126)

Return to your car and continue to Tyne Cot British Cemetery. The largest Commonwealth war cemetery in the world is not part of the tour but is worth a visit. It contains more than 12,000 burials of Commonwealth service men, of which 966 are Canadian. Of the Canadian burials, 554 are unidentified.

Return to Ypres via Zonnebeke or, preferably, return to the main road and go to Ypres via Passchendaele, Westrosebeek and Poelcapelle. Observing the battlefield from the heights occupied by the Germans adds an interesting perspective.

CEMETERIES AND MEMORIALS
Of the Battle of Passchendaele,
October-November 1917

The numbers are shocking. The remains of more than 600,000 Commonwealth servicemen lie buried in some 3,500 cemeteries carved quaintly into the rolling hills and farmers' fields of northern France and Belgium.

Landscaped and constructed during the 1920s by the Imperial War Graves Commission (now the Commonwealth War Graves Commission), these cemeteries have frozen the history of the First World War.

The principles of the IWGC, established in 1917 to maintain the cemeteries and record the Commonwealth[15] dead of the Great War (and later the Second World War), were threefold:

1) The name of each serviceman who died in the war or during the immediate postwar period would be commemorated on a headstone or engraved on a battlefield memorial.

2) All would receive universal treatment in death.

3) No bodies would be repatriated. All would remain in the country where they died.

The repatriation restriction and the acquisition of the land where the cemeteries originally stood have preserved for perpetuity the legacy left by the hundreds of thousands who sacrificed their lives in foreign lands.

CEMETERY CATEGORIES

The types of cemeteries fall into three main categories:

I. HOSPITAL CENTRE CEMETERIES are near main hospital centers or casualty clearing stations. All burials are in chronological order and few graves are unidentified. The officers usually have a separate burial plot, as do Hindus, Moslems and Buddhists.

---

[15] The term Commonwealth applies to countries of the old British Empire, namely Australia, New Zealand, India, Pakistan, Canada, South Africa, Britain and other British colonies or protectorates.

Servicemen of the Jewish faith are usually buried in the Christian plots but there are exceptions. In Etaples, a plot for black soldiers (generally of the British West Indies Regiment) includes one Canadian.

II. REGIMENTAL OR FRONT-LINE CEMETERIES are cemeteries near the front lines for quick burial of soldiers killed at the front (trench wastage) or small battlefield cemeteries set up by Divisional or Corps Burial Officers immediately after a battle. Often the layout and rows are irregular.

III. BATTLEFIELD CLEARANCE CEMETERIES were usually small cemeteries greatly expanded after the war by the concentration of remains brought in from surrounding battlefields. They always contain a very high proportion of unidentified graves and the layout of the rows is regular and often symmetric.

The nature of the Passchendaele fighting precluded the honored or normal burial for the majority of those who died in battle. German artillery was ferocious even after the battle ended and putting men's lives at stake for those already dead was not reasonable. Consequently, many dead remained where they fell, in shell holes, or were absorbed into the sucking mud. Only those who died of their wounds had the honor of a known burial.

In 1919, when the battlefield clearances started, 25,000 bodies of Commonwealth soldiers were found in the area north, south, and east of Passchendaele. Most were found in solitary, unmarked graves. More than 70% were unidentifiable in spite of the dual identification tag system introduced in late 1916.

Parties searching the battlegrounds of 1914 and 1915 also found most of the remains were unidentifiable. The body of Brigadier-General Riddell of the Northumberland Brigade, killed in the Second Battle of Ypres on April 26, 1915, was initially labeled as an unknown Brigadier General!

All these bodies were concentrated into several cemeteries in the area. The cemeteries containing most of the Canadian burials killed in the Passchendaele battle are listed below.

THE MENIN GATE MEMORIAL

The Menin Gate Memorial is on the eastern edge of the old town of Ypres on the road to Menin. It was built in the 1920s to

Ypres. The Menin Gate, 1919

(PUBLIC ARCHIVES OF CANADA - PA 4618)

commemorate Commonwealth soldiers killed in the Ypres Salient and who have no known grave. Engraved on its walls are the names of more than 55,000 Commonwealth soldiers, including 6,983 Canadians. The names are listed by unit, rank, then alphabetically.

The Canadians named on the memorial were killed predominantly in the battles of Second Ypres 1915, St. Eloi 1916, Mount Sorrel 1916 and Passchendaele 1917. Roughly two thirds of the men killed at Passchendaele have no known grave and are commemorated on the Menin Gate.

The officers apparently learned their lesson by 1917. Note that three high ranking officers were killed at Ypres in 1915, four at Mount Sorrel in 1916 and none at Passchendaele in 1917. Major Talbot Papineau's name heads the list of the missing of the Princess Patricia's Canadian Light Infantry.

Listed on the panels of Menin Gate are the names of three Canadian Victoria Cross winners. Lieutenant Hugh Mckenzie VC, DCM, won his VC posthumously at Meetcheele on October 30, 1917. The other two, both killed at Ypres in 1915, are Company

Sergeant F. W. Hall, VC, of the 8th Canadian Infantry and Lance Corporal F. Fisher, VC, of the 13th.

The memorial, designed by Sir Reginald Bloomfield, was unveiled in 1927. Every night at 8:00 p.m., traffic on both sides of the memorial comes to a halt while buglers of the Ypres Fire Brigade sound The Last Post. This is a very moving experience.

TYNE COT BRITISH CEMETERY

Tyne Cot Cemetery is the largest Commonwealth war cemetery in the world. Started in 1917, with the irregularly laid out original burials north of the cross of sacrifice, the cemetery lies three kilometres southwest of the village of Passchendaele. Concentrations from the battlefields during the searches between 1919 and 1921 enlarged the cemetery considerably.

It contains 11,871 war graves, of which 70 percent are unidentified. Of the 966 Canadians in the cemetery, 554 are unidentified. Nine hundred graves are those of Canadians killed in the Passchendaele fighting of 1917.

Plot 58, Row D, Grave 26 contains the remains of Private James P. Robertson, VC, of the 27th Battalion (City of Winnipeg), who won his Victoria Cross posthumously for bravery on November 6, 1917 during the capture of Passchendaele village.

The graves of two Australian Imperial Force soldiers who were awarded Victoria Crosses posthumously are also buried here. Captain C. S. Jefferies of the 34th Battalion was killed October 12, 1917 and Sergeant Lewis Mcgee of the 40th Battalion was killed October 13, 1917. They are buried respectively in Plot 40, Row E, Grave 1 and Plot 20, Row D, Grave 1.

The names of British and New Zealander soldiers killed in the Ypres Salient with no known grave are engraved on the back wall of the cemetery. The British soldiers missing in the salient after August 15, 1917 and the New Zealanders missing in the October 1917 fighting are commemorated here.

PASSCHENDAELE NEW BRITISH CEMETERY

Passchendaele New Cemetery is on the road to Gravenstafel north of Passchendaele. The cemetery was made in 1920 and 1921 from battlefield clearances and contains 2,091 Commonwealth burials of which 77 percent are unknown. Canadian burials number 650; 452 (70 percent) of them unknowns. The cemetery location is significant as it rests on the Bellevue Spur at Mosselmarkt.

All Canadian burials are casualties of Passchendaele. In 1991, reexamination of original documents led to the identification of four previously unknown Canadian soldiers: Lieutenant E. C. Platt of the 24th Battalion, killed November 7, 1917; Lieutenant R. C. Gillespie of the 72nd Scottish Highlanders of Canada, killed at Crest Farm October 30, 1917; Captain C. T. Costigan, DSO, MC, of the 10th Battalion (Alberta), killed November 11, 1917 (identified by medal ribbons on his tunic); and Private L. O. Millership of the 2nd Battalion (Eastern Ontario), killed November 6, 1917 (identified by a penknife engraved with the initials L.O.M. found when his remains were discovered in 1921).

POELCAPELLE BRITISH CEMETERY

Poelcapelle is nine kilometres northeast of Ypres on the Ypres-Roulers highway. The cemetery lies in open country east of the village on the road to Westroosbeeke and was made in 1919 and 1920 from the clearances of the battlefields. It contains the graves of 7,469 Commonwealth soldiers, 83 percent unidentified. Almost all the burials are those of soldiers killed in the Battle of Third Ypres 1917.

Of the 525 Canadians in the cemetery, 80 percent are unidentified. Four hundred of the Canadians were killed at Passchendaele. Most of them were with the Canadian Mounted Rifles units and involved in the northern flank of the Canadian attack of November 6-10, 1917. Plot 28, Row E, Grave 3 contains the remains of Lieutenant Allen Otty of Gagetown, New Brunswick. He was killed in the valiant and successful attack of the 5th Canadian Mounted Rifles at Source Farm on October 30, 1917 and led by George Pearkes. It seems unjust that Pearkes won the Victoria Cross for his bravery while Otty received no recognition for his courage. He was 29.

Lieutenant Major Tutzer "MacCohen" Cohen, MC, of the 42nd Black Watch of Montreal, was killed at Graf House on the night of

LANGEMARK GERMAN CEMETERY

The dead of many nations lie buried in cemeteries all along the Western Front. The cultures of these diverse nations are reflected in the styles of the national cemeteries. The Commonwealth cemeteries, designed on the concept of Edwardian gardens, contain the graves of soldiers from Britain, Ireland, Australia, New Zealand, South Africa, India, Canada, Newfoundland, Ceylon and the British West Indies. There are also Portuguese, Italian, Russian and American cemeteries. All are different but, in general, reflect their victory.

On the other hand, the German cemeteries are unique in design and ambiance. Langemark, just north of the village of Langemark and the only German cemetery in the Ypres Salient, is a forbidding and eerie graveyard built over and around the German Flanders defence line of 1917. Typically German, it is a dark, sombre place, the sadness and malignancy of war the more so emphasized by statues of elongated mourners, pillboxes, dark stonework and shade trees.

The cemetery was completed in the mid-1950s to amalgamate the many smaller German cemeteries concentrated around Ypres. Six kilometres northeast of the town of Ypres, it now contains the remains of 44,294 soldiers. More than 24,000 of them are buried in mass graves, each marked with a recumbent plaque. One of those 24,000 is a known British soldier who died as a prisoner-of-war in Roeselare and whose remains were removed through an administration error to Langemark. A headstone in Roeselare Communal Cemetery memorializes this soldier.

In April 1915, the Germans launched their first poison gas attack on the French lines 500 metres east of the cemetery.[16]

---

[16] See For King and Empire Vol. I: The Canadians at Ypres, April 1915.

November 3, 1917. He was 22 and from Toronto. His remains are buried in Plot 34, Row A, Grave 15.

This rarely visited cemetery is perhaps the one that most represents the Third Battle of Ypres. Sad and isolated, only 1,300 of the 7,500 men killed in a sea of mud have a name. The other forgotten heroes rest in oblivion or, as their headstones explain, "Known unto God."

DOCHY FARM NEW BRITISH CEMETERY, LANGEMARCK

The cemetery is found on the road from Zonnebeke to St. Julien. Gravenstafel Ridge, the New Zealand monument (at the Gravenstafel crossroads) and the Passchendaele church are visible in the middle distance to the west of the cemetery. Tyne Cot Cemetery is to the right.

The cemetery was used after the war to bury remains found during the battlefield clearances of 1919. It contains the graves of 1,437 Commonwealth soldiers including 81 Canadians (48 unidentified). Only 33 percent of the graves have been identified. All the Canadians died in the Battle of Passchendaele, the majority between October 26 and 30, 1917 while serving with the 4th Canadian Division.

OOSTTAVERNE WOOD CEMETERY, WYTSHCAAETE

The cemetery is south of St. Eloi on the road to Lille (Rijsel in Flemish). It is predominantly made up of remains found by search parties, farmers or flying squads during the battlefield clearances of 1926 and contains 1,119 graves (70 percent unidentified) of which 133 are Canadian. Thirty of the Canadians here died in the Passchendaele fighting.

BUTTES NEW BRITISH CEMETERY, ZONNEBEKE

Buttes Cemetery is two kilometres south of the village of Zonnebeke in a wood known as Polygoneveld or Polygon Wood. The cemetery was made from battlefield clearances in 1919. Commonwealth graves number 2,066, of which 81 percent are unidentified. Fifty graves contain the remains of Canadians, all killed in the Passchendaele fighting, the majority 4th Canadian Division killed between October 26 and 30, 1917. Only six are identified.

Ypres Reservoir Cemetery

(S. HICKMAN)

YPRES RESERVOIR CEMETERY

The cemetery is an easy walk northeast from the Grote Markt in the center of Ypres. It was used continuously throughout the war and enlarged by the battlefield clearances. It now contains 2,611 Commonwealth graves, including 151 Canadians. The Canadian soldiers were killed in a variety of battles between 1915 and 1917. Roughly half are graves of those killed in the Passchendaele fighting.

Of interest are the graves in Row H of Plot 1, which contain the remains of twenty men of the 123rd Canadian Pioneer Battalion killed by one shell on October 21, 1917. Private W. Tobias of that unit was an Indian chief from the Brantford Reserve. Buried in Grave 76 in that row is Private Thomas Moles of the 54th British Columbia. Moles was executed for desertion and one of 25 Canadians executed in the Great War.

One Victoria Cross winner is buried in the cemetery. Brigadier General Francis (Frank) Maxell, VC, DSO, commanding officer of the 27th Brigade of the 9th (Scottish) Division was killed by a sniper on September 21, 1917. His Victoria Cross was awarded for bravery during the Boer War, 1899-1902. He is buried in Plot 1, Row A, Grave 37.

THE HOSPITAL CENTERS:

LIJSSENTHOEK MILITARY CEMETERY, POPERINGHE

The second largest Commonwealth War Cemetery in Belgium is two kilometres south of Poperinghe in open country. This area was the direct communication link with Ypres throughout the war. A light gauge railway was built between the two towns to transfer supplies, munition, and reinforcements to the front and to withdraw casualties. As Lijssenthoek was near the railway siding, wounded were brought there from the salient throughout the war.

Typical of a hospital center cemetery, the men are buried in chronological order and virtually all are identified. The officers have been buried in their own plot. It contains 9,829 Commonwealth burials, of which 1,051 are Canadian.

WILLIAM JOSEPH BLACKBURN

PRIVATE, *1st Canadian Mounted Rifles, C.E.F.*

Was born in Manitoba on September 29th, 1896. After completing his education in Holylea School, he entered the service of the Bank of British North America at Oak River, Manitoba, at the age of eighteen. He enlisted in November, 1915, as a Private in the 90th Battalion. He proceeded overseas with his unit and after a further period of training in England he arrived in France in 1916, being attached to the 1st Battalion, Canadian Mounted Rifles. He went into action with his battalion in the Somme sector where intense fighting was then in progress, but he passed unscathed through the battles in which his unit was engaged in 1916 and the greater part of 1917. After serving for over a year in the line he was severely wounded by fire during an attack upon an enemy position. He died from his wounds on November 15th, 1917.

GEORGE BASIL BROWN

ACTING CORPORAL, *Canadian Field Artillery*

Was born in Toronto, in 1898. He received his education at Ashbury College, Ottawa, and after graduation he entered the service of the Bank of Montreal. In December, 1915, he enlisted as a Gunner in the 32nd Battery, Canadian Field Artillery; he went overseas with his unit and after a brief period of training in England he arrived in France in the following May. He took part in all the battles in which the Canadians were engaged during 1916 and 1917, on the Somme, at Vimy Ridge, at Hill 70, and in the Ypres salient. For gallant and distinguished conduct during the attack for the capture of Vimy Ridge on April 9th, 1917, he was awarded the Military Medal. He was instantly killed by enemy fire on November 14th, 1917, during the Canadian offensive for the capture of Passchendaele Ridge in front of Ypres.

The Canadians buried here represent minor and major actions in which Canadians participated in the Ypres Salient between 1916 and 1917, particularly Mount Sorrel and Passchendaele. Fatalities from the latter are predominantly buried in Plots 21 through 27.

Buried in Plot 6, Row A, Grave 38 is Major General Malcolm Mercer, CB, commander of the 3rd Canadian Infantry Division. Killed at Mount Sorrel June 2-3, 1916, Mercer's body was not found for more than three weeks because of the chaotic conditions. He was the highest ranking Canadian soldier to die in the war.

NINE ELMS BRITISH CEMETERY, POPERINGHE

Nine Elms Cemetery is directly off the ring road around Poperinghe, on the western side of the town. Similar to Lijssenthoek, it was a hospital center specifically set up for the Third Battle of Ypres. It contains 1,556 Commonwealth burials, of which 289 are Canadians. They are all Passchendaele casualties and are buried in Plots 5 through 9.

VLAMERTINGHE NEW MILITARY CEMETERY

Vlamertinghe is five kilometres west of Ypres. The cemetery is two kilometres south of the village of Vlamertinghe. It is a typical hospital center cemetery used predominantly for wounded from the Third Battle of Ypres. It contains 1,813 Commonwealth burials, of which 155 are Canadian. The Canadians are buried in Plots 9 through 12.

A Scottish Victoria Cross winner is buried in Plot 13, Row H, Grave 15. Company Sergeant Major John Skinner, VC, DCM, of the Kings Own Scottish Borderers, was killed by a sniper on March 17, 1918. His Victoria Cross was awarded for bravery in the Third Battle of Ypres 1917.

Further Afield

The following cemeteries, along the northern coast of France on the English Channel, are major cemeteries associated with all Canadian actions between 1915 and 1918. All are typical hospital center cemeteries with burials in chronological order, few unknowns and a separate plot for officers and nurses.

WIMEREUX COMMUNAL CEMETERY

Wimereux is seven kilometres north of Boulogne. The cemetery was used from 1915 to 1918 and contains the graves of 2,847 Commonwealth soldiers, of which 216 are Canadian. The Canadian burials reflect many battles, but particularly Vimy and Passchendaele. At the entrance of the cemetery is a memorial plaque to Lieutenant Colonel John McRae, Canadian Army Medical Corps, who died on active service (of pneumonia) January 1918. He is most famous for the poem, In Flanders Fields, he wrote at Ypres in 1915. He is buried in Plot 4, Row H, Grave 3.

Due to ground instability, all the First World War headstones are recumbent.

BOULOGNE EASTERN CEMETERY, FRANCE

Boulogne is 100 kilometres west of Ypres on the English Channel coast. The cemetery is in the city's eastern sector above the harbor on the road to St. Omer. It was used for hospital burials from 1914 to 1918 and contains 5,578 Commonwealth burials, of which 442 are Canadian. The Canadian burials reflect various actions between 1915 and 1918, including Ypres, Mount Sorrel, the Somme, Vimy and Passchendaele.

Of interest is the grave of Captain Frederick W. Campbell of the 1st Canadian Battalion (Western Ontario). Campbell died on June 19, 1915 of wounds received in the battle of Festubert on June 15. His Victoria Cross was awarded for conspicuous bravery at Festubert. He is buried in Plot 2, Row A, Grave 24.

ETAPLES MILITARY CEMETERY

Etaples Cemetery is on the coastal road between Boulogne and Le Treport, three kilometres north of Etaples. It was used throughout the war and contains 10,729 Commonwealth graves, including 1,123 Canadians. This cemetery reflects the Canadian losses during the major actions of Mount Sorrel, the Somme, Vimy, Passchendaele and the Advance to Victory.

Etaples was the major depot base for the British army on the Western Front and was the location of the infamous Bull Ring and the British mutiny of 1917.

On May 19, 1918, German Gotha bombers made direct hits on the No. 1 Canadian General hospital, killing 66 people, including three nursing sisters. The men killed in the attack are buried in Plots 66, 67 and 68. The nursing sisters are buried in Plot 28.

Other cemeteries containing Canadian burials of the Battle of Passchendaele are:

CEMENT HOUSE CEMETERY, LANGEMARCK

TRACK 'X' CEMETERY

LA BRIQUE CEMETERY No. 2

NEW IRISH FARM CEMETERY

ARTILLERY WOOD CEMETERY

HAGLE DUMP CEMETERY

BRANDHOEK MILITARY CEMETERY

SANCTUARY WOOD CEMETERY

HOOGE CRATER CEMETERY

STE. MARIE CEMETERY, LE TREPORT, FRANCE

ST. SEVER CEMETERY EXTENSION, ROUEN, FRANCE

THE BODY SNATCHERS

The love a mother felt for her son drove her to dig up the body of her beloved and "bring it home" eight years after his death.

William Arthur Peel Durie was born in Toronto in 1881, son of Dr. and Anna Durie of St. George Street. Like many affluent gentlemen of his era, Durie took up a career in banking and a commission in the local militia unit, the 36th Peel Regiment.

In 1915, the 34-year-old enlisted in the 58th Canadian Infantry and went to France in March 1916. On May 4, he was seriously wounded by a sniper bullet and almost died of his wounds. Incredibly, he recovered and rejoined his unit in France in December.

On December 29, 1917 in the frontline trenches near Lens, a large trench mortar shell hit the parados, killing Durie instantly. He was buried in Corkscrew British Cemetery near Lens, France.

In 1919, his mother Anna approached the Imperial (now Commonwealth) War Graves Commission (CWGC) and asked about repatriating the body. Her application was rejected. In August 1921, determined to have her wish, Anna, her daughter and a Frenchman made an unsuccessful nocturnal attempt to remove the body from the cemetery.

In August 1925, when all the graves in Corkscrew Cemetery were exhumed and moved to Loos British Cemetery, Anna took advantage of the shuffle to remove her son's body. Although the ground disturbance was noted by the CWGC, a ground probe determined the coffin to still be there. The CWGC did not find out about Anna's nighttime prowl until a Toronto newspaper reported the reburial.

William Peel Durie, 1915

Her son's grave is in St. James Cemetery, Toronto. He was buried with full military honours with ex-soldiers of the 58th Canadian Infantry in uniform attending the ceremony.

What brought Anna to France also brought many other families to France and Belgium during the 1920s to search the battlefields for the lost grave of a loved one. Learning a husband or son was "missing" only accentuated the tragedy and sorrow brought to more than a million British Commonwealth families by the First World War. Of the 1,115,000 Commonwealth dead (66,000 Canadians), more than 530,000 had no known grave. Under the terms of the CWGC, no bodies were permitted to leave the country in which the man had died. For Canadian families, then, few of their loved ones would be buried at home.

Some families were not satisfied with this condition and applied for repatriation of the body. The application was always refused. The alternative left to the bereaved family was to steal the body from the military cemetery and ship it home for reburial. Between 1919 and 1925, hundreds of thousands of bodies were dug up and reburied in war cemeteries. Old battlefields still scarred the fields and the chances of getting away with a clandestine operation were great. Local help could even be purchased to assist.

It is not known and is difficult to estimate how many bodies were removed in this fashion. CWGC records indicate only six such thefts, but appear to overlook others, for example, the famous heist of the South African Fighter Ace Captain Andrew Beauchamp-Proctor VC, DSO, MC, DFC from his original grave in England. Of the six recorded thefts (three were Canadian), four were successful.

Private Grenville Hopkins of the Princess Patricia's Canadian Light Infantry (PPCLI) was killed November 15, 1917. In 1920, an unmarked grave containing two bodies was found north of Passchendaele village. The two were Private Granville Hopkins and Private McKeown of the PPCLI. The father of Private Hopkins identified the remains of his son. In January 1921, the family applied for repatriation of his remains, but the application was denied. On the night of May 17/18, 1921, the body was removed and the theft discovered the next morning. Belgian authorities were alerted and the body was found in the mortuary in Antwerpen and reclaimed.

Private Hopkins is now buried in Schoonselhof Cemetery. His parents are long dead.

Major Charles Sutcliffe, a Canadian in the Royal Flying Corps, was killed June 6, 1917 and buried in Epinoy Churchyard in France. In August 1925, a man accompanied by Sutcliffe's father had the body exhumed and taken to Canada. Major Sutcliffe is now buried in Lindsay, Ontario.

The question of repatriation remains an issue today. Only the Australians have been successful. After the First World War, the remains of Major General Sir William Bridges, KCB, CMG were repatriated from his burial place in Egypt to Australia. In 1994, the Australian government repatriated an unknown soldier from a CWGC cemetery in France.

The Israeli government has tried unsuccessfully to repatriate men of the Palestine Regiment killed in Italy during the Second World War. Fiji tried unsuccessfully to repatriate a Fijian Victoria Cross winner from a cemetery in Papua, New Guinea.

In the 1970s, the Republic of Ireland requested the repatriation of three soldiers of the Connaught Rangers, buried in India, whose graves had been abandoned by the CWGC. As the graves were no longer within the jurisdiction of the CWGC, all three were repatriated to Ireland and reburied as heroes of the Irish Nationalist cause.

The only legitimate repatriations took place after the Second World War. Foreign nationals who died serving in the Commonwealth forces could be repatriated if the request was made officially by the non-Commonwealth country to which the soldier was a citizen.

LAUNCELOT EDWARD CARTER

PRIVATE, *43rd Battalion, C.E.F.*

JOHN FRANCIS MALONEY

LIEUTENANT, *21st Battalion, C.E.F.*

Was born in Camden Town, London, England, on July 23rd, 1885. He received his education in the schools of his native city and in Beccles College. He joined the staff of the Bank of British North America in London in 1905, and after two years of service there he was transferred to Canada. He was stationed in several branches, and was ultimately promoted to be Manager of the branch at Saltcoats, Saskatchewan, where he was employed at the time of his enlistment. He enlisted in February, 1916, as a Private in the 174th Battalion, Cameron Highlanders of Canada, and after some months of training in England he went to France with a reinforcement draft for the 43rd Battalion. He was killed in action in the Vimy sector on November 11th, 1917, just after his battalion had moved south from Passchendaele.

Was born in Calgary, Alberta, in December, 1896. He received his education at the schools of his native city and at Ottawa University, and after leaving the university he entered the service of the Bank of Montreal. He enlisted in June, 1916, as a Gunner in the 72nd Battery Depot Ammunition Column, but he transferred later to the Canadian Infantry, in which he received his commission as Lieutenant. After completing a qualifying course and training for some months with his unit he went overseas in March, 1917, with a reinforcement draft for the 2nd Battalion, but on arriving in France in August, 1917, he was attached to the 21st Battalion, Canadian Infantry. A few weeks after he reached the firing line he was killed in action at Passchendaele on November 9th, 1917, the day before the final attack for the capture of the village and the ridge.

CANADIAN INDIANS

Chris Silversmith was typical of many Canadian Indians who served in the Great War.

He was born on the Six Nations Reserve at Caledonia, Ontario. They never recorded the date of birth, but he was apparently 26 years old when he enlisted in 1916 with the 114th Battalion at Caledonia. His enlistment documents indicate the strapping 6'3" Silversmith's religion as Long House - Pagan and it is clear the enthusiastic farmer could not sign his own name. His complexion is noted as 'dark Indian', his hair 'black', his eyes 'very dark'.

Half of the 114th and the 107th Battalion of Winnipeg were made up of Indian recruits. Clearly sympathetic to the Canadian Indians, the officers of the 114th still had that age-old unmalicious prejudice against inferior races so prevalent in the British Empire. However, unlike other races, the Canadian Indians were recruited with genuine interest because of their reputation as a daring and loyal "warrior" breed.

Most of the 3,500 Indians who enlisted were scattered throughout the forces. They represented tribes from across Canada including the Micmacs, Mohawks, Onondagas, Oneidas, Tuscaroras, Delawares, Chippewas, Sioux, Bloods, Okanagan, Peguis, Saulteaux and Crees. Among them were the famous long-distance runner Tom Longboat; Cameron Brant, great grandson of Joseph Brant; and Patrick Riel, grandson of the Metis leader Louis Riel.

Once in England, the 114th Battalion was broken up for reinforcements and sent to France piecemeal. Silversmith was sent to the 107th Canadian Pioneer Battalion and fought in the battles of Passchendaele and Hill 70, where he was wounded.

Others served as snipers or scouts. Henry Norwest was considered to be the greatest sniper in the British Army and was credited with 115 "observed" hits.

Although clearly successful soldiers, the "lesser race" prejudice remained. When the Military Service Act was introduced in 1917, the Indians were excluded because they were "wards of the Government and, as such, minors in the eyes of the law, and that, as they had not the right to exercise the franchise or other privileges

Private Chris Silversmith, convalescing in England, 1918

of citizenship, they should not be expected responsibilities equal to those of enfranchised persons."

Nonetheless, more than 35 percent of eligible Canadian Indians enlisted. A tremendous percentage! By the end of the war, they had won 30 awards for bravery. The most decorated of all was Francis Pegahmagabow of Parry Sound, who was awarded the Military Medal three times.

They had also instilled fear in the enemy. Legends of Indian stealth, cunning and ferocity were world-renowned. A German soldier captured at Vimy recalled:[17]

"...the English were all over us. I walked up the steps behind a corporal who was very defiant and he spat on the floor... but this did him no good for he was hit over the head by a huge tommy who was brandishing a baseball bat... Looking at the soldiers I noticed that they all had their faces blackened...

"One of the soldiers wore no helmet and had no hair apart from a small tuft on the top of his head. He also had white and red paint on his face and was very fearsome looking. I then realized he was a Red Indian, and our captors were Canadian."

Unfortunately, more than 320 Canadian Indians died in the war or as a result of war service. The first to fall was Cameron Brant, killed at Ypres in 1915. Patrick Riel fell late in 1915, the victim of a sniper's bullet. Even Henry Norwest, the intrepid sniper, was finally sniped himself in August 1918. The revered marksman was buried by his comrades in Warvillers Churchyard, east of Amiens.

Like other Canadian soldiers, these men returned to Canada in 1919 to a strangely different world. In the series, "Canada in the Great War," the following passage expresses their future hopes:

"The unselfish loyalty, gallantry, intelligence, resourcefulness and efficiency displayed by Indians from all nine provinces of Canada should throw a new light upon the sterling qualities of a race whose virtues are perhaps not sufficiently known or appreciated.

"The Indians themselves moreover cannot but feel an increased and renewed pride of race and self-respect that should ensure the

[17] Excerpt from "Cheerful Sacrifice" by J. Nicholls, Leo Cooper, 1990

recovery of that ancient dignity and independence of spirit that were unfortunately lost to them in some measure through the depletion of the game supply, their natural source of livelihood and the ravages of vices that has no place in their life before the advent of the white man.

"The Indians deserve well of Canada and the end of the war should mark the beginning of a new era for them wherein they shall play an increasingly honourable and useful part in the history of a country once the free and open hunting ground of their forefathers."

Silversmith was injured in 1918 and evacuated to England. He returned to Caledonia in May 1919 but fell ill and his death on March 25, 1923 was attributed to war service. He is buried at Cayuga Long House Reserve, Caledonia.

Chris Silversmith left a wife, Catharine, and two daughters, Ida and Emiline. He was "apparently" 33 years old.

IS IT NOTHING TO YOU ALL
YE THAT PASS BY

The sacrifice of the Great War was felt in all communities, large and small, across Canada. Each community wanted to offer its own token of respect in memory of the fallen. Many towns formed committees of local veterans from the Great War Veterans Association and women from the Imperial Order of the Daughters of the Empire, local clergymen and businessmen to come up with the right way to show reverence.

Poet Rudyard Kipling was one of those involved. Kipling penned two verses for Canadian monuments at Sudbury and Sault Ste. Marie. The Sault Ste. Marie verse is especially poignant:

In little towns in a far land we came,
To save our honour and a world aflame.
By little towns in a far land we sleep;
And trust that world we won for you to keep.

In most cases the community decided to erect a war memorial in a central location, a place of honour, to remember the dead. Money was quickly raised by private donations. During the 1920s, war memorials were a thriving business as cenotaphs, cairns, obelisks, slabs, statues, pillars, gates or crosses were erected.

The unveiling ceremonies, usually on Remembrance Day, were the focus of an important community function and continue to this day.

Many of the surnames on the memorials in the smaller communities live on in distant relatives but, to a large extent, the "real people" named, the "unforgotten dead," are not remembered. The sacrifices of those who came before, poignantly understood years ago, have primarily been lost to a lack of knowledge.

A Northern Ontario town memorial at Thessalon, a community of 1,700 people, stands in a prominent position beside the

Thessalon War Memorial

Thessalon River which runs through the town. The monument lists the names of 31 local men who died on the field of honour.[18]

LEST WE FORGET

CHARLES BARKLEY *Private Charles F. Barkley, 156th Canadian Infantry. Born December 21, 1896. Son of Mike Barkley. Farmer. Enlisted at South Mountain, Ontario. Died of disease in England March 21, 1917.*

ANGUS BEATON *Private Angus Beaton, Military Medal, 58th Canadian Infantry. Born at Day Mills, Ontario January 31, 1895. Son of Sam Beaton. Beekeeper. Died of pneumonia March 1, 1919. Buried in Edinburgh, Scotland.*

JOHN BELL *Private John Alexander Bell, 58th Canadian Infantry. Born at Goldenburg, Ontario October 30, 1889. Son of Neil and Janet Bell of Bellingham, Ontario. Stationary Engineer. Killed in action March 24, 1918.*

NEIL BELL *Private Neil Cameron Bell, 58th Canadian Infantry. Brother of John Bell. Farmer. Killed in action August 27, 1918.*

WILLIAM BOOTH *Private William Francis Booth, 58th Canadian Infantry. Born on St. Joseph's Island February 9, 1895. Son of William and Louisa Booth of Nestorville, Ontario. Killed in action August 26, 1917. Buried at Aix-Noulette, France.*

JAMES COLE *Private James Stanley Cole, 19th Canadian Infantry. Son of David and Annie Cole of Thessalon, Ontario. Died of a gunshot wound to the abdomen August 29, 1918. Buried at Ligny-St. Flochel, France.*

FRED DOBIE *Lance Corporal Fred Dobie, Princess Patricia's Canadian Light Infantry. Killed in action May 7, 1916.*

CLIFFORD ELDER *Private George Clifford Elder, 116th Canadian Infantry. Born at Bobcaygeon, Ontario June 16, 1888. Son of G. M. and*

---

[18] Sadly, most war memorials required extra space for the names of the fallen of the Second World War. On the Thessalon memorial, two columns listing 17 local men were added after the Second World War

Jennie Elder of Hudson Bay Junction, Saskatchewan. Cook at Nestorville, Ontario. Killed in action at Cambrai October 1, 1918.

SYDNEY FERGUSON *Private Sidney John Ferguson, 52nd Canadian Infantry. Born at Maniwaki, Quebec May 28, 1894. Son of Alinda Ferguson of Maniwaki. Blacksmith. Severely wounded in the stomach by enemy shrapnel on August 15, 1918, died the following day.*

ROBERT FORBES *Private Robert Spence Forbes, Canadian Machine Gun Corps. Born at Belfast, Ireland February 16, 1891. Lived at Livingstone Creek, Ontario. Husband of Mary Anne Forbes of Thessalon. Wounded in the eye and shoulder at Passchendaele on November 14, 1917. While being evacuated he was instantly killed by the explosion of a shell.*

ERNEST GRIFFITH *Sapper Hugh Ernest Griffiths, Canadian Railway Troops. Born at Thessalon August 8, 1895. Son of Richard and Mary Griffiths of Thessalon. Sailor. Died of a penetrating shrapnel wound to the chest October 13, 1917.*

HENRY HAMILTON *Private Henry Edward Hamilton, 85th Canadian Infantry. Born at Thessalon. Brother of Myrtle Hamilton of Sowerby, Ontario. Marine Fireman. Died of influenza December 7, 1918.*

CECIL HARRIS *Private Cecil Harris, 13th Canadian Infantry. Born at Webbwood, Ontario July 16, 1896. Son of Mrs. T. A. Harris of Thessalon. Hotel man. Killed in action April 19, 1916.*

ERNEST HODDER *Private Ernest George Hodder, 58th Canadian Infantry. Born at London, England May 13, 1887. Son of Mary and Joseph Hodder. Bookkeeper. Shot in the head by an enemy sniper near Cambrai on September 30, 1918, killed instantly.*

THOMAS JORDAN *Private W. Thomas, Canadian Infantry Reserves. Born at Wyevale, Ontario June 26, 1896. Son of Mrs. W. Jordan of Little Rapids, Ontario. Farmer. Died at sea en route to England, October 14, 1918. Buried at sea.*

RUSSEL KIRBY *Private Russel Lawrence Kirby, 102nd Canadian Infantry. Born at Dane Mills, Ontario September 10, 1897. Fireman. Son of Thomas and Georgina Kirby of Dayton, Ontario. Severely wounded in the leg by a piece of shrapnel on September 3, 1918, succumbed the following day.*

ARTHUR MCALPINE   *Private Arthur McAlpine, Princess Patricia's Canadian Light Infantry. Born at Gore Bay, Ontario November 14, 1880. Salesman. Son of Gilbert and Nettie McAlpine of Thessalon. Missing June 2-4, 1916.*

ROBERT MCDOUGAL   *Private Robert George McDougal, Canadian Machine Gun Corps. Born Goldenburg, Ontario January 12, 1892. Motorman. Son of Mrs. R. McDougal of Thessalon. Instantly killed by the explosion of an enemy shell at Passchendaele on November 10, 1917.*

LAWRENCE MIRON   *Private Lawrence Miron, Canadian Machine Gun Corps. Born at La Lavre, Michigan May 29, 1894. Son of Julia Miron of Nestorville. Instantly killed by the explosion of an enemy shell on August 26, 1918.*

FULTON OLIVER   *Private William Fulton Oliver, 116th Canadian Infantry. Born at Londesboro, Ontario October 3, 1894. Farmer. Husband of Christina Oliver of Thessalon. Killed in action August 28, 1918.*

RUBEN PEACHEY   *Private Reuben Edward Peachey, 102nd Canadian Infantry. Born at Collingwood, Ontario April 28, 1895. Mason. Son of William Peachey of Thessalon. Killed in action at Passchendaele October 30, 1917.*

EARL SANDIE   *Private Earl Clayton Sandie, 116th Canadian Infantry. Born at Thessalon March 13, 1898. Clerk. Son of James Sandie of Thessalon. Instantly killed by an enemy bullet near Cambrai on September 29, 1918.*

ALLEN SEABROOK   *Private Hugh Allen Seabrook, Canadian Machine Gun Corps. Born at Meaford, Ontario June 2, 1893. Farmer. Son of James Henry and Eliza Jane Seabrook. Killed by a bomb dropped from an enemy plane while on parade September 24, 1918.*

THOMAS SHEPHARD   *Private Thomas Sheppard, Forestry Corps. Born in London, England June 28, 1886. Lived in Thessalon. On October 13, 1917, he was driving a logging truck full of logs when the truck jolted. He was thrown to the ground and crushed by the falling logs.*

ROY SHEWFELT   *Private Roy Godfrey Shewfelt, 58th Canadian Infantry. Born at Baysville, Ontario July 1, 1898. Son of William and*

Harriet Shewfelt of Thessalon. Mortally wounded in the head and body by shrapnel near Arras August 27, 1918.

ROY SHOULTZ *Private Roy Watson Shoultz, Canadian Machine Gun Corps. Born At Listowel, Ontario July 7, 1892. Son of Henry Shoultz of Thessalon. Killed September 24, 1918 with Hugh Seabrook.*

HARRY STYLES *Private G. Harry Styles, Canadian Machine Gun Corps. Born at Arnprior, Ontario July 21, 1890. Nephew of Anson Styles. Killed in action July 31, 1918.*

FRANK VALLEY *Private Frank Valley, 52nd Canadian Infantry. Born Gaspé, Quebec January 14, 1888. Father of Raymond and Narresse. Missing, presumed dead September 3, 1917.*

JOHN WILSON *Corporal John Wilson, Canadian Engineers. Born at Shetland, Scotland September 8, 1885. Son of Elizabeth Wilson. Died of disease February 5, 1919.*

GEORGE YOUNG *Private George Irwin Young, 102nd Canadian Infantry. Born at Calendar, Ontario November 17, 1897. Son of William and Josephine Young of Thessalon. Killed in action September 23, 1917.*

FOR FURTHER REFERENCE

This guide has focused solely on the actions of Canadian troops in the Battle of Passchendaele 1917. However, the infantry at Ypres far exceeded that battle. Thousands of Canadians were killed at the Second Battle of Ypres in 1915, at Mount Sorrel in 1916 and while holding the line from Ploegsteert to Hooge in 1915 and 1916. The salient would be a curse throughout the war for troops of all nationalities.

Today, the Ypres Salient is the largest burial ground in the world. The monuments and cemeteries of the British, French, Belgians, Germans, Australians and New Zealanders are densely scattered throughout the salient. Many deserve a visit.

I have outlined below several books that will greatly increase understanding of the "immortal salient":

Before Endeavours Fade, by R. E. Coombs (the best guide book on the Western Front), Battle of Britain Prints International, 1976.

Ypres, Then and Now, by J. Giles, Leo Cooper Ltd., 1970.

Ypres and the Battles for Ypres 1914-18, Michelin Guide, 1919.

They Called it Passchendaele, by L. MacDonald, MacMillan, 1978.

Legacy of Valour, by D. Dancocks (the Canadians at Passchendaele), Hurtig, 1986.

Welcome to Flanders Fields, by D. Dancocks (the Canadians at Ypres 1915), McClelland and Stewart, 1988.

Beyond Courage, by G. Cassar (the Canadians at Ypres 1915), Oberon Press, 1985.

The Official History of the Canadian Expeditionary Force 1914-19, by G. W. L. Nicholson, The Queen's Printer, 1962.

Tapestry of War, by S. Gwynn (excellent coverage of the PPCLI at Bellewaerde 1915 and Mount Sorrel 1916), Harper Collins, 1992.

Australian Battlefields of the Western Front 1916-18, by John Laffin, Kangaroo Press, 1992.